T0082866

It Wasn't My Shame

A Story Of Survival And Healing

Alice Edwards

authorHOUSE®

AuthorHouse™
1663 Liberty Drive
Bloomington, IN 47403
www.authorhouse.com
Phone: 833-262-8899

© 2022 Alice Edwards. All rights reserved.

No part of this book may be reproduced, stored in a retrieval system, or transmitted by any means without the written permission of the author.

Published by AuthorHouse 04/18/2022

ISBN: 978-1-6655-5671-2 (sc)
ISBN: 978-1-6655-5670-5 (e)

Library of Congress Control Number: 2022907020

Print information available on the last page.

Any people depicted in stock imagery provided by Getty Images are models, and such images are being used for illustrative purposes only. Certain stock imagery © Getty Images.

This book is printed on acid-free paper.

Because of the dynamic nature of the Internet, any web addresses or links contained in this book may have changed since publication and may no longer be valid. The views expressed in this work are solely those of the author and do not necessarily reflect the views of the publisher, and the publisher hereby disclaims any responsibility for them.

This book is lovingly dedicated to my wonderful husband. Without you I would have never been able to brave the path I have walked. I am forever grateful for your unconditional love and unwavering belief in me. You and me, Me and You, forever and ever.

And to my beautiful boy. I am so proud of the amazing human you are becoming every day. You will always be my inspiration.

I love you both in unspeakable amounts!

Finally, my ever-faithful companion. To some you may be only a dog. But you are My dog. I am ever grateful for your unending snuggles and your big goofy smile!

This story is my memoir. It reflects the story from my recollections and viewpoint. Names have been changed, some events have been compressed, and some dialog has been recreated to protect the innocent and the guilty.

Dear Little Alice,

My sweet girl. I have put off writing this letter for an exceptionally long time. Mostly because I was not sure what to say. And, if I am being honest, I still don't. I want to start by telling you that I see you. You have never been hidden from me. I see how strong you are and how strong you have always been. I know how hard you have always tried to protect those you love from hurt or harm. I know how quietly you suffered. I see how hard you worked to be good and quiet and to stay out of the way. I see how hard you strive to earn the pride of those around you. I see how hard you work to earn their love and admiration. I see each tear that your blankie has collected. I see each time you inflicted pain on your own body to release the pain you felt inside your soul.

I see how abandoned you feel. I understand the grief and the outrage you feel that the people who were supposed to love you, protect, and even treasure you, chose to satisfy their own selfish needs instead. I see how you feel abandoned by a god that you gave your whole soul to. I was there when you poured your heart out to that god in the wee hours of the night. How you begged for hope and help, for protection and solace, just to be met with an overwhelming silence.

I see the walls that you built brick by painstaking brick around your soul. I see the gate as tall as the sky that keeps your love inside and everyone else outside.

I feel the way you tremble. I feel your heart race and your breath come short. I feel your frustration that you just can't be normal. I am with you and have been with you, every step.

But today I am here to tell you, it's ok. You are safe. I have you. You don't have to be stuck in that dark, cold basement anymore. You don't have to be afraid of who is sneaking around your door. No one will ever sneak into your room, ever again. No one will peek at you. No one will ever use your body or your spirit for their own personal gain. No one will ever hurt you to make themselves feel good. Ever again.

I see you now. You are kind and strong. I see you in my glittery earrings and my tie-dye hair bows. I hear you when you sing rap songs at the top of your lungs and when you giggle at a fart joke. I see you being the mom you wish we had when you snuggle with Leo. I see you being vulnerable with the people around you, how you reach out in compassion. I see how you love Grant with an ever-growing and always-learning love. I am so proud of you!

Our life is beautiful. With Grant's unwavering love and support you are healing and growing stronger every day. You are breaking the cycle of abuse, neglect, and unkindness. You are teaching your son how to live with kindness and compassion before anything else. You are teaching him to be strong and advocate for himself and to be a voice for those who cannot speak for themselves.

You are becoming the person who you needed all those years ago.

This is the part where I tell you all is well. It is safe for you to go play now. But I am not ready for that yet. I want you here with me. I want you to experience the joy of being safe and loved unconditionally. I am going to hold you for a little while longer. I understand that there are still things to grieve. I understand there are still times to be angry and sad. That's ok. I've got you. I won't leave. Even if you stumble and take a few steps back, I will still be here. Just please don't give up. Keep going. You have fought so hard and survived too much to give up.

I love you.
I see you.
You are a good girl.
I am proud of you.
Always, Always,
Adult Alice

Chapter 1

The first interaction with my dad, that I can remember, happened when I was 10 years old.

We had moved to Springfield, Missouri, so my parents could attend a Christian College. They were heeding the Lord's call for them and for our family to eventually become missionaries to some foreign field, perhaps in the Philippines. So, we left Indiana and everything we knew behind.

I know that there were people around. I have faint memories of people, adults, and kids at the apartment. I'm not sure why. However, there were always people around. Friends of my brother's, college kids my parents took under their wing came over to study or just hang out, families from church over for dinner and fellowship. We always seemed to have a full house. Kids running up and down the stairs. Lots of noise, laughter, and distractions.

The apartment we lived in was actually a townhouse. It had two bedrooms and a full basement. The basement was home to the laundry room as well as my brother's room. We also played down there a lot. We liked to clear the floor and roller skate on the bare concrete.

Growing up, there was always teasing. Some in good, wholesome fun, some not. Dad was always wrestling, tickling, or teasing me.

During one tickling session, dad lifted me up and sat me on the top of the dryer. He continued to tickle and tease me. And then with both arms on either side of me, he asked "Do you want me to show you how mommy and daddy kiss?" I gave a tiny shake of my head no, more from confusion than anything. This didn't feel right. What was happening? Was I in trouble? Would I be in trouble? What was the right answer? Kids weren't supposed to do what mommies and daddies do, but we weren't supposed to tell mommy and daddy "no" either.

While I was trying to figure out the situation, Dad leaned in and kissed me on my lips. We never did that in our family. My mom had been adamant all my life that only mommy and daddy did that. Sometimes Nanny and Poppy kissed me on the lips, but they were old and that's just what old people did. And while I was trying to wrap my head around this wave of thoughts, dad stuck his tongue in my mouth.

That was super weird. It made me feel sick to my stomach and my knees feel like Jell-O. I wanted out of there.

I jumped off the dryer with a nervous shrug and ran outside with the rest of the kids.

Chapter 2

Growing up, I missed the bus one time. It was in the sixth grade, and it never happened again. After that 10-minute drive to my middle school from our apartment, I knew I couldn't let it happen again. I would just as soon as walk the six miles before I would ask my parents for a ride ever again.

It was my responsibility to get myself up, showered, dressed, and to the bus stop on time. I was 11 years old. Forget breakfast. I didn't even know kids actually ate breakfast before school. I thought that was just on my favorite family sitcom.

I ran as fast as my short legs would carry me to the bus stop at the entrance of the apartment complex. But, when I got there, all I saw were taillights. I stood watching them disappear. I walked the several blocks back to our apartment in the cool morning air, heart heavy with dread.

I was scared to wake my parents up. I knew I would be in trouble. I hated getting into trouble. I hated to make mistakes. I prided myself on making everything in my life right, straight, neat, and on time.

I had failed.

I climbed the steps to my parents' bedroom, trying with each step to think of a different solution. I knew my mom would be no help, she didn't have a license and couldn't drive. With a deep breath, I pushed their door open a crack and quietly said, "Dad. I'm so sorry, I missed the bus." With a huff and a muttered "Good grief, Alice," my mom shook my dad awake. "Stan, she missed the bus, you will have to take her to school." Dad worked third shift and came home at 4 a.m. He hadn't been asleep long and had classes of his own that morning. The lecture about my selfish, irresponsibility began as soon as his feet hit the floor.

My dad and I got into the cab of the little red pickup truck that we were borrowing from a friend. I remember pushing myself against the windows to be as small as possible.

I wasn't allowed to wear pants and culottes were far from trendy and sure to make me the punchline of the "cool kids" jokes, so of course I had on a jean skirt. No matter how much I inched away, Stan's hands still found my leg and inched up my thigh. My stomach clenched as he pulled off onto a country road that I knew was not the way to school. I kept reminding him I was going to be late. If I were tardy, I would lose my perfect attendance award.

Stan told me not to whine, "You won't be that late." He pulled down the waist band of his sweats and putting his hand on the back of my head, he pushed my head down into his lap.

15 minutes later, I signed my tardy slip while swallowing down tears and bile and rushed to my homeroom

Chapter 3

We had been in the church since I was in the first grade. Meaning saved, baptized, every time the doors open, "Here I am, Lord, send me," *in* the church. But around fourteen, I started to take it seriously. Instead of it just being the way I was raised, it was the way I lived.

I understood in my mind what it meant to accept the gift of Jesus's crucifixion to atone for my sins. It made sense to me even as early as the first grade that if I could simply say a few words and not spend eternity in a Lake of Fire, it would be a fairly wise idea to say those words. I didn't feel the tug or calling in my heart though. However, on a trip to Kansas for my dad's preaching engagement, something changed. We went to a park where a traveling Christian college drama group were putting on skits and plays in the amphitheater. This really wasn't anything that incredible. These types of things were a part of daily life growing up on a Christian college campus.

As they began the last skit of the day, something caught my attention. The opening notes of "Total Eclipse of the Heart" began to play. This was different. The actors began to surround the girl who was the main character. On their shirts were written various issues that surround teens. Drugs, sex, peer pressure, etc. The circle closed around the girl. They began pushing her, closing in on her, not letting her out. She became increasingly distressed. All of this to music, no dialogue. And then as the girl fell to the ground defeated, a big strong man broke through the circle and picked her up, carrying her to safety. I heard faint sobs. Looking around I realized the cries were my own. My dad led me away and I confessed that I wanted to be saved. I wanted that relief of rescue. Ironic, isn't it? That the one leading me to the rescue, was the one I needed rescued from?

From that moment on, salvation became a lifestyle for me. Not just my parents' religion. I dedicated my life to learning and practicing the lessons of Jesus. I joined the choir, worked on the bus ministry as a bus captain, taught children's Sunday school, taught vacation Bible school, joined the Bible quiz team, and mentored young girls. Whatever I could do to be a part of reaching, teaching, and loving people the way Jesus did.

Not only did I try to reach people with my newly found faith, but I also thought surely the Bible must hold the answer for me as well. I spent hours reading, noting, and highlighting my Bible. I would pull out my parent's textbooks, the Concordance which weighed almost as much as I did.

My brother and I were alone a lot while our parents were at school and then working remodeling houses together. I would spend those hours searching for answers. Crying out to God to fix me. To make me holy, to cleanse me. To point out what inside of me was making this happen. I would do whatever it took to make it better.

I would beg for God's forgiveness every night after my dad would leave my room.

"I am so sorry, so sorry. Please forgive me. Please cleanse me. Please make me better. Please don't turn your face from me." This was my nightly plea. Over and over until my eyes could no longer cry and I would finally sleep.

Chapter 4

Christmas 1998

When I was thirteen years old, I wanted a CD player for Christmas. Our family of four came "home" to Indiana from Missouri. I loved going home. Seeing my family felt safe. I slept on the sofa at Nanny and Poppy's house. There was no way my dad would risk being caught. In my mind, that meant a whole week of peace. But I was wrong. It wasn't a risk; it was a challenge.

In this tiny, little house that had always been my sanctuary. While my grandparents slept in their room off the kitchen behind a flimsy vinyl accordion door, I could hear my poppy's snores as my dad crept down the stairs into the living room where I slept. On the second night, I felt the all too familiar presence hovering over me, the trembling in my belly as I woke to his fingers on my thighs. There was no sanctuary.

Our visits home could sometimes be a minefield of drama due to dividing time between each side of our family and friends. The same argument would always arise around which family had spent more time with us than the other. This year there was an addition to the tried-and-true dispute.

My Papaw, Stan's dad, and his new wife had recently moved back to Indiana. Stan Sr. didn't have a great reputation or relationship with us. He was in and out of our lives even more than he was his own kids. But Papaw was settled and was trying, so we were all gathering for dinner.

I don't remember why, but mom didn't come with us that night. It was known that my mom didn't particularly like or enjoy the company of Stan's side of the family. She tolerated my grandma, but really didn't put a lot of effort into the relationship with my Papaw or Stan's siblings. There was a time when we were all close, but religion gave her the excuse to pull away from this side of the family even more. My dad's family were not overly religious. Christmas was a celebration, so they would drink a couple of beers, smoke cigarettes and play cards. All these things were considered un-Christian like and should be avoided. It was still odd looking back that she didn't come with us. Perhaps she was exercising a rare moment of independence.

It was late when we made our way to Stan Sr.'s. I was excited, I really enjoyed the times we did see Papaw. There was always music and if we were really lucky, everyone would pull out their guitars and play and sing. Music was my life.

I was nervous because I wouldn't have mom with us. At the time, I felt having her with us was security. It wasn't. But still, even then, we were in someone else's home with family members sleeping in every room, there is no way that my father would come for his nightly visit. Right? Wrong.

I remember Stan was almost giddy after he stopped at a Dollar Store on the way. I didn't pay attention. I was just ready to get to the food, the music, and the laughter.

It was a great night. It felt like a normal, fun, family night. I fell asleep to the sound of the adults laughing over their card game.

Several hours later, Stan woke me up. Usually, I did everything in my power to pretend to still be asleep. I thought, no matter what, don't let him know you are awake. If you aren't awake, you don't have to participate. Just close your eyes, steady your breath, and wait for him to go away. Not this night, Stan was insistent.

He took me into a spare room filled with old dusty treadmills and an exercise bike.

Stan pulled out a small bottle of baby oil, the reason he stopped at the Dollar Store. He wanted to give me a massage. Dad said this as if it was a gift or a special treat.

The room was dark and cold and I was completely naked in front of him. This was the first time. This was before all the times my dad snuck in while I was showering for his little sneak peeks. I trembled violently as his rough and calloused hands ran over my thin limbs with the slick oil. Every fiber of my body recoiled in disgust. I wanted to scream. I wanted to push his hands off me, but I was paralyzed by my upbringing. You don't tell Daddy "No." What would he have done if I had screamed? What would have been the punishment of which I was so afraid? Would my aunt and uncle had rushed in?

I don't know. I can't fathom. I had no power. It never crossed my mind that I could fight back or say no.

This is the first and rare time that my mind turned off. Shut me down and saved me from whatever the rest of the massage entailed.

Chapter 5

My little brother and I rode the church bus to Sunday school faithfully every Sunday for many months. One Sunday in particular, we had a campaign that the pastor called "Round Tuit Sunday." Our teachers handed all the children small wooden tokens, these were round tuit tokens, declaring: "Your parents have told you every week they would come to church with you when they get around to it, so now they have one." The gathering of lost souls being the main and most important goal, with a reward being given to the child who brought the most visitors. To my surprise, my parents actually came.

Later in our Christian life when my mom would give her testimony, she would speak to the fact that their marriage had become very strained. My parents would talk about a feeling of being at loose ends, tired of their lifestyle, they would say they were searching for something to fulfill them. They needed a higher purpose. So, they rode the church bus to Sunday school with their children.

I didn't know or understand any of that. I was just a little girl excited to show off her parents at church. It would seem that my parents found what they had been searching for because life began to change in many ways after that first Sunday.

The first change consisted of our family's church attendance. Our family now attended church the way good Baptists should: Every time the doors were open. We not only attended now, but we got involved. Within a few short months of attending, my parents were singing in the choir, counseling younger married couples, and teaching the Junior and High school kids' Sunday school classes.

Slowly, things that had been normal activities and routines, changed. The music we listened to, the books we read, the movies we watched, even the places we went to and the people we associated with, Including certain family members. As time went on, my parents became increasingly "convicted" of different ideals.

Each Sunday seemed to end with one or both parents at the altar confessing and repenting parts of their lives. These altar calls ultimately led to changes in our lives.

One of the verses that my parents quoted daily was from 1 Corinthians 8:13. Now I will quote the New International Version for purposes of clarity. However, I must take this time to point out that our church was even specific to the proper version of the Bible, which could be no other version but the King James Version.

1 Corinthians 8:13 says "Therefore, if what I eat causes my brother or sister to fall into sin, I will never eat meat again, so that I will not cause them to sin."

In this passage, Paul is speaking to the Corinthians, encouraging them to love and edify one another. That even if something isn't necessarily bad or sinful but would offend or cause another person to falter or waiver in their faith, it then becomes sinful. This passage was used to justify both minor and extreme instances in our life. For example, if a restaurant advertised as a "bar and grill" or had beer signs in the window, we wouldn't frequent those places. Someone that we had been trying to convert may drive by and see us in the window and wouldn't know if we had ordered a beer or not but may think we have, and that could put a doubt in their mind regarding our faith. Or they may drive by a movie theater advertising rated R movies and see our car in the parking lot and assume that we are watching an ungodly movie, this again would lead to doubts in our loyalty to Jesus.

Our church prided itself on being literalist. Meaning they taught that the Bible translated literally into our lives. So literally, if drinking Pepsi instead of Coke offended one of our brothers in Christ, we were to stop drinking that soda. We were expected to be living Bibles to the world. We were commonly told that we "may be the only Bible some people will ever read." It was our job as Christians to guard everything we said, did, and consumed to be as Godly as possible.

This was especially true for all females, including young girls. At church they began segregating us by gender as early as the fifth grade. We began to have separate Sunday school classes and were commonly separated for activities. Our teachers began to stress to us young girls the importance of being pure and lady like, to be careful and modest. It was important to protect ourselves, but most important to protect our young brothers in Christ from stumbling into lustful thoughts.

As young girls, our church began to teach us that we were created specifically to be a helpmeet to men. We were meant to train ourselves in the way of wives. Until God gave us a husband, we were to be a helpmeet to our fathers and brothers.

We were taught that during creation, God took out the rib of Adam specifically to make a woman who would assuage Adam's loneliness. The literalist leaders in our church translated that to mean: Women were created for the sole purpose of men, whatever their purpose may be.

That is a very heavy lesson for a young girl to grasp. To know that my life's purpose had been boiled down to simply meeting the needs of men. No one ever went as far as to teach us that we were less than men or less important than men. Instead, they used words like meek, submissive, dutiful, and modest.

The lesson was that men and boys have so much in their lives to focus on growing into and being men of God, leading their churches and families, that they are susceptible to impure thoughts and actions. These are things that are not in ***their*** control, but ours. It is our duty to not only dress modestly but to speak in higher pitched, quiet voices, so as not to trigger their ears with sultry tones. To dress with every inch covered above the elbow and below the knee to not trigger their eyes with our flesh. To guard our conversations and to speak on only Godly things so as not to trigger their brains with seductive thoughts. This was our job, our duty, and our purpose.

A common lesson that we were given at our teen nights was of the rose. As a teen girl there is nothing more magical and enchanting than a red rose. Roses are the symbol of romance and beauty. The church leaders would invite a guest speaker to the event who would usually be a good looking, charismatic, young man, with hip haircut and cool clothes. He would look like he wasn't much older than us. He would be the kind of guy that all the girls would want to marry and that the boys would want to become.

The young pastor would hold up the beautiful rose and admire all of its qualities. Then he would hand it down from the stage to the closest teen in the crowd. He would instruct us to admire the color, the velvety petals, smell the fragrance, then pass it to the next person. As you can imagine after passing through the hands of two hundred or more teenagers, the delicate rose begins to look rough by the time it makes it back to the preacher on stage. Petals are falling off, the stem may be broken, the edges of the remaining petals turning brown. The young preacher now holds up the broken rose and says "This is a young lady's heart after she has given it away to multiple boys before she gives it to the man God has chosen for her. Which rose would you want? The pure, whole, and beautiful rose or the broken, smashed, and dirty rose?"

There are many variations to this lesson; chewed gum, used tape, bruised apple, or a brand-new bike that the neighbor has ridden and returned broken. In all these analogies, the takeaway is that a girl's heart and body is an object defined wholly by her sexuality, while the boys are still human beings capable of making conscious choices.

Most importantly, these were lessons to encourage young girls to guard themselves against the wayward thoughts of boys, because boys were not capable of controlling themselves. However, if there was a mishap, if something impure did happen between a boy and a girl, it was the girl's fault. By being immodest, she caused the mishap. Something impure could be as simple as hand holding or kissing, to the extreme of sexual acts and loss of virginity.

The idea was to stress the importance of protection, however, what we as young teens took away was shameful. Everything pertaining to our physical body became nothing more than a vehicle for sin. It felt shameful simply to be a young girl going through the natural state of puberty.

The lessons of purity culture led to shame which turns into secrecy and then grows into ignorance. When even the basic development of your body is seen to be shameful and dirty, you can no longer have open conversations about these things. When there are not open conversations, there is no education.

In our family, I wasn't even allowed to attend sex education in health class when I was in public school. In fact, at the beginning of every school year until my parents removed me from public school, my dad would come in and meet with my teacher and go through each textbook. If there was a lesson that he felt did not adhere to our doctrinal belief, for example evolution or sex education, I would be excused from class and sent to the office. Even if it meant not passing that class. I would have to work harder in other areas to average out those failing grades.

So, these teens aren't learning about their bodies at home or in school. Not only does this lead to confusion, but also to secrecy and shame.

It leaves teens and even young children without the knowledge and language to protect themselves in the instance of abuse. We cannot tell you what is happening or where we are being hurt if we don't know.

Another very confusing and harmful lesson we were taught by our doctrine was that "sin is a sin is a sin." Confusing, right? The concept is that any indiscretion is sinful. There is not one sin any worse than another sin in the eyes of God. The crucial story for this lesson is a familiar one to most people. During the crucifixion of Jesus there were two criminals on either side of him. One mocked him and one begged his forgiveness. Jesus at once forgave the one who asked and extended the invitation to Heaven. So many times, in my life I have heard this story referenced with the addendum that it did not matter what crimes that man had committed in his life, by turning to Jesus, even in the end, he was forgiven. This translated down to us to mean that disobeying your parents, smoking cigarettes, doing drugs, drinking alcohol, cussing, stealing, sex outside of marriage (at any age), and even murder were all equal sins in the eyes of God.

Here is why I feel this is a destructive theology: when there is no progression of misdeeds to a worsening degree it leads to an inability to decipher and determine your standing in society. For example, when a child is experiencing abuse, especially of a sexual nature, it is hard for them to decide that that is a reason for alarm because they will feel as if they are judging and casting blame because the sins in their personal lives are just as detrimental. Moreover, young women especially are at risk for this thinking due to the emphasis put on their sexuality and the idea that if a man misstep it is due to something they did to tempt him, or in the place of his wife, something she didn't do to meet his needs.

Many times, we find that victim blaming becomes extremely common in the fundamentalist environment. There is an umbrella of protection, starting with Jesus Christ and narrowing to the wife of a family. It is commonly taught that if you step out of that umbrella of protection and something happens to hurt you, it is ultimately on your shoulders. There are issues with that type of thought. First, there is never a justification for assault or abuse to any gender or age group. Secondly, it is often used as an excuse for perpetrators and those who choose to stand beside those perpetrators. Stepping out from the umbrellas can be anything from listening to a song that makes someone want to dance, to wearing a skirt above the knee or reading a provocative book.

There are many lessons I learned from the theology and doctrine of the religion of my childhood. It shaped who I am as a person in many ways, good and bad. There is much good that the church is capable of. However, I also feel there is much room for improvement and accountability. The double standard of many of the teachings of the fundamentalist environment can and will only lead to continued abusive patterns that produce fractured people.

It is the duty and responsibility of the church, as a body of authority, to contribute to the raising and healing of the people it serves. I understand that the goal of the church is to open the eyes of the world to a life after death, however, we have an overwhelming number of people from all levels of society who are experiencing a life of sorrow and hurt, due in part to the confusion, toxicity, and venom in the teachings of the church.

Chapter 6

Anger was an ocean tide in those days. It ebbed and flowed. Some days it flooded my soul and left me without words, without breath. I felt as if I was silently screaming into the void.

Other days were blanketed in clouds of despair. Sadness fell from my eyes like hard pelting rain.

Guilt and shame were my constant companions. They bracketed my days like bookends.

I was shattered before I had a chance to be whole.

Can you even begin to imagine the torture and turmoil of a young girl growing up at the height of purity culture being routinely molested? By her father? By the one set by God himself to guard that purity and innocence?

The trend at this time was to present young teen daughters with a ring to represent their commitment to remain pure. For my twelfth birthday, my parents gave me my purity ring. A tiny 24-karat gold ring with a heart and cross and a small chip diamond. It stayed on my left ring finger for many years and mocked me with its tiny beauty and meaning. I wanted to be proud of it. It was so pretty. But I knew in my heart it represented so many lies.

My abuse began at the beginning of puberty. At this time, my dad made it seem as if it was normal, that he was training me to be a woman. It was many years later that I realized this was completely abnormal behavior. At this time in my life, I was so sheltered and had very few friends my own age, so I had no frame of reference for normal family life.

As I grew older and the abuse continued, I remember my dad saying this was his way of protecting me. With him, my heart and body would be safe, my heart because I wouldn't give it to just any boy and my body because he would never "go too far" or hurt me.

If any temptations should arise when I was with my boyfriend, I should come to my father, that way my purity would stay intact. A girl without her "purity" was a girl unfit for a godly husband. We were taught that giving not only our bodies away, but also our love, would make us damaged goods and no godly husband would want a damaged wife. Our entire lives and everything we were taught was about making ourselves worthy to become wives of godly men.

My Dad told me that if I came to him with these temptations, my heart would remain pure and whole. His words didn't matter. My soul knew, my heart knew. I was forever damaged goods.

He was my father. Obedience had been ingrained in me. "Do what you are told, when you are told and with the right heart attitude." This definition was taught to me from as early as six years old. One of the first things I ever memorized.

I did not say no, I did not know I could. No, had never been a choice in my life. I tried to resist in my own ways.

I had mastered pretending to be asleep. Not just simply keeping my eyes closed but evening out my breathing and making my body completely limp. It didn't matter. My dad would move my arms, legs, and hands to do his bidding.

After I began shaving my legs in the sixth grade, I would go weeks without shaving, which doesn't seem like a big deal for such a young girl, except I wasn't allowed to wear pants, only skirts and knee length culottes to public school. This was before the days when Christian teen girls could make basketball shorts work as modest. I had very thick dark hair on my legs. It was a big deal. I thought my dad would find it gross or unappealing.

It didn't matter.

I also started my period in the sixth grade. I knew what was happening from reading Judy Blume's "Are you there, God, it's me Margaret?" Other than that, no one had told me how these things worked. I wasn't allowed to participate in the part of health class where they showed the film and talked about these things, so I was clueless. I was so embarrassed; I even hid the fact I started my period from my mom.

For a week I would have peace. I thought if I just continued wearing pads to bed, he would notice and leave.

Obviously, my dad knew more than I did about how female bodies work. He knew periods didn't last three weeks.

Chapter 7

One common lesson of the Bible can be found in the Book of Joshua from the Old Testament. When the Israelite army were losing battles, Joshua called upon the lord and God told him there was "Sin in the camp."

Anyone who has spent any time in the Baptist Church will probably be familiar with this lesson.

It was my dad's favorite. He could preach it loud and fiery for adults and would even make a Kool-Aid version for kids.

The essence of this story is the idea of "sin in the camp." God had told the Israelites to touch nothing, but *one* soldier chose to disobey and in doing so brought God's wrath down on everyone in the camp. Even today, many years later this story has the power to make me weak with self-doubt. The idea that something *I* had done wrong could cause a whole congregation of people I cared about to miss out on blessings God had for them because of a secret sin. My father would preach this, railing on and on about secrets and hidden sins. How those secrets were holding back our families, our church. How everyone was affected and hurt by our secrets. But I knew. I knew what he did the night before or sometimes the same afternoon. The sin was his, but both the guilt and the shame fell on me.

Every time he preached this message, I found myself drawn to the alter. I would kneel and sob, begging God to forgive me. To make me clean. Promised my heart, my soul, my life if God would only forgive me.

It wasn't until years later that I would realize, it was not my sin as I was not the one in control. The man standing above me was. Stan would stand at the pulpit watching *me* cry and beg forgiveness for *his* sin.

On my shoulders, I carried his sin.

In my hands, I held his shame.

Chapter 8

A friend of my parents had graduated from A Christian Bible College and was accepting a position at a church in Kansas. They couldn't fit all their furniture in the moving van, so they asked my parents if I would like to have their daughter's old full-size mattress. Furniture of any kind was hard to come by on our family's income, so we were happy to inherit any upgrades.

No more twin bed for me. My room was going to look like a teenager's room. I was so excited. We got the mattress moved upstairs and my new bed setup. A couple of weeks later, one of the Sunday school teachers at the church pulled my mom aside. She had sat behind me in Sunday school and noticed I had lice. I was mortified and beyond embarrassed.

My hair wasn't long and I was very conscious of having short hair and looking like a boy. Also, as in most churches, the longer the hair, the closer to Jesus. Hair was a woman's glory. I always kept my hair in a cute, but shorter than popular, chin length bob. Even though I was excited for a teenager's room, I was still very much a little girl. I had a huge stuffed animal collection, everything from Disney characters to fuzzy cats. If it was cute and plush, I had it. These animals had been my constant companions my whole life and at times my only friends. I would circle them around me in a nest at night, like tiny stuffed centurions to protect me from monsters, imagined and real. Putting those little stuffed bodies in dark trash bags broke my heart. I actually marked the 30 days out on the calendar until I could bring them back upstairs. Another part of the solution was to cut my hair as short as possible. Thankfully, my parents didn't shave my head and allowed me to go to a salon. The beautician cutting my hair tried her best to be kind. I remember she went through the haircut as quick as she could without raising any concerns. I was burning with shame as I sat in her chair.

We battled it for six weeks until discovering they were coming from the mattress.

Worst of all of it, someone suggested mayonnaise and saran wrap. At this time, Stan worked third shift at a factory building transmissions. So, while he was at work, mom slathered my head and wrapped it in plastic. To comfort my miserable self, she said I could make a pallet on the living room floor and watch tv until I fell asleep.

At 4 a.m. and even in the middle of the living room floor with my head covered in mayonnaise, I felt the familiar crawl of his hands across my bare tummy under my pajamas.

Even all these years later, I can recall the feeling of absolute defeat and shame in the pit of my soul. My only thought was "Even now.."

Chapter 9

On the outside, we looked and behaved like an average Christian family. Even those closest to us would never have imagined what went on behind closed doors. There were times when the edges of what happened the night before softened in the warmth of the laughter of the good days.

The secret was always there. Pulling like an undertow. The amount of work I put into being and appearing normal was exhausting for such a young child. But there were a few times when the darkness faded, even for just a moment. The times when we just existed, shared laughs, and made memories.

As a kid, I didn't know that we were different. I thought our parents loved us because this was the only way I had ever felt or experienced love. As an adult and a parent, I know now that our parents loved us. However, they made us fit into their lives rather than our family *being* their life.

Most Saturdays we would pack a cooler, fishing gear, and a book for mom and I and head to a lake, creek, or river to fish and explore.

I remember one of the spots we liked to frequent had huge slabs of limestone in the creek. My mom, brother, and I would walk up the creek a little away from where my dad was fishing. One slab of stone was slippery with moss and created the perfect slide into a babbling pool of ice-cold creek water. It was hard to stay on our feet, so we slid. Even my mom. We giggled and slid down that slab of stone until our butts were sore and the chill of the creek water made us shiver even in the summer sun.

My mom and I share a love of reading and libraries. The best days of my childhood were spent at the library. Our very first priority when we moved to a new town or even a new neighborhood was to find out how far the library was and if we were lucky, it would be within walking distance. We would take tote bags and backpacks with us to carry home our borrowed treasures. The rest of those evenings were spent exploring the worlds within those books. Escaping reality, as cliché as that sounds, to a world where I could be a conqueror, a brave explorer of faraway lands, or an investigator solving crimes and mysteries.

When my dad worked construction, we would all pile in the car and travel with him to surrounding towns. While he built houses, we explored the libraries in those towns.

My mom and I also liked to go shopping at dollar stores. We loved to see what cool things we could discover for just one dollar. Especially snacks. I have always loved junk food. Even in foster care and now as an adult I always keep snacks around me.

I remember one year for my parents' spring break, we took a family trip to Arkansas. We were home schooled by then, so we didn't have to worry about missing school.

We swam in the hotel pool and shopped. We even went to a magic show! Magic was a huge taboo for us. One of the many weird things we didn't participate in because of church doctrine. I am not sure if these beliefs came from the church or just my dad's interpretation.

My brother and I inherited my dad's sense of humor and all three of us would go out of our way to make my mom laugh until she couldn't breathe or would pee her pants.

We loved to go to basketball games at our local Bible College. There is nothing more fun than a college basketball game. There is live band music, cheerleaders, and the smell of popcorn! When I was fourteen, I even volunteered to help in the concession stand. That was an intense experience for a shy, homeschooled girl. I got nervous ordering my own food or asking for ketchup at a fast-food restaurant. At the time I might as well have been swimming with sharks instead of counting change and serving hot dogs to college kids. At the biggest game of the season, we were so busy we ran out of soda. We had to change out the soda concentrate boxes. Neither one of us working that night had any idea what we were doing. We ended up getting showered in orange soda.

My parents did their best to take us home to Indiana for the holidays. My brother and I laughed and argued the whole five hundred miles. I loved "going home." Not just because we saw family and friends, but I loved the long car rides. I loved riding in the backseat watching the world go by and imagining all the possible lives a person could live.

One year, we were snowed in at Nanny's house. There was more snow than I had ever seen. My dad shoveled a path to the family's house that lived down the street from Nanny's. We had been friends all our lives, and my parents had been since they were in high school. The snow shoveled pathway allowed us to go over there to hang out and play games. But the highlight was when we got to see not one, but two movies in an actual movie theater! My dad finally agreed because we were so bored and had run out of things to do and games to play.

Movie theaters were another huge taboo in the Baptist circles we were in. I wish I had an explanation of why. The closest I have to an explanation is we were taught to not be "stumbling blocks" to people around us. If someone walked by and saw we were attending a movie they might think we were seeing a movie that had crude and indecent themes and that would not be a good Christian example. Whatever the reasoning was, my dad decided that this one time, due to extreme boredom, we could go and watch a movie at the old movie theater. We watched *A Bug's Life* and *Prince of Egypt*. The second movie led to a month-long family Bible study on Moses. However, the movie theater popcorn was definitely worth it!

Another one of my favorite memories was when my mom managed a small residential home for elderly ladies with Alzheimer's. Since we were not in traditional public school, we spent our entire day there with her. I loved helping with the ladies and hearing their stories. One lady used to love to watch us rollerblade in the parking lot. We would play music on the radio and skate around. She would clap and shout "Bravo, what a beautiful performance." For Thanksgiving that year, we decided to stay and spend the holiday with the ladies in the home instead of going back to Indiana. To this day that is one of my favorite Thanksgiving meals.

Looking back, I feel like my parents loved me because that was their job. But my brother and I were accessories to their lives. My parents always made it known that they came first in each other's lives. Their love for each other would always supersede their love for us.

The love we did share as a family is now colored by the reality of the abuse and neglect. It is hard to look back now and see things clearly without looking through the lens of adulthood.

They always say hindsight is 20/20.

Chapter 10

Growing up, my parents were strict. Well, Stan was strict; my mom just followed his lead. Even before we started going to church, we were expected to behave a certain way.

I don't know at exactly what age I learned that the smaller and quieter I could make myself, that the less attention I required, the easier my life would be.

The overall theme of my childhood was "Alice is as good as gold," "she is so quiet, we almost forgot she was here." I was a quiet and well-behaved child. But those golden child behaviors were the result of a fear of punishment and a greater fear of disappointment.

I had this desire to hear my parents proclaim their pride over me. I sought similar gratification from other authority figures in my life such as grandparents, aunts, and teachers. As a young girl, before I recall the abuse beginning, I would easily be called a daddy's girl. I wanted so much for him to be proud of me. To tell me that I was smart and capable, my mom too. But I also feel looking back that there was no way to compete with my brother. In her heart, Bobby was hers and I was Stan's. That is simply how it felt.

As I grew older, my mom and I became close, but it was a forced closeness in the beginning. As a teenager, I clung to her, likely in search of rescue. I will always wonder how she did not see the signs and if she did, how she managed to turn her back and pretend she didn't.

There are children who cry out for attention, I was not one of them. From an early age I entertained myself with stories I made up. As a young child I didn't just have an imaginary friend, I had an imaginary village of friends to keep me company along with my collection of stuffed animals and dolls.

My mom used to say that I could rarely have more than one friend. I wasn't mean, but I was bossy. Even as a small child, I wanted to be perfect. I wanted all rules to be followed. *I* had to follow the rules.

I searched for ways to control my environment. If you keep things in order, follow the rules and stay quiet, you don't get in trouble. You are a good girl.

I never wanted anything more than to be a good girl.

Chapter 11

The last time my father touched me was a week before I told Levi my secret. It had been a terribly busy weekend. We had been moving into our new house late into the night on Friday. On Saturday we woke up early and hit the road to a nearby theme park with the youth group. I was happy and excited to get to hang out with my friends and ride roller coasters with Levi.

We had a blast! We were allowed to break off into small groups and get out from under the eyes of the adults. It was great to be able to act like a normal teenager and hold Levi's hand while we strolled through the park.

My group consisted of my best friend Brooke, Levi's best friend Blake, and of course, Levi and me. We rode every single roller coaster and water ride. The group made a big deal about making me stand in front of the "are you tall enough?" chart. It was a running joke with everyone that we would only be able to ride kiddie rides because I was so short. Levi and I shared a milkshake with two straws. Blake teased him all day about that. Levi just laughed it off. I remember him saying "Just wait until you love a girl. Nothing else matters but her smile." It was a wonderful day.

The next day after church we ate lunch as a family just like normal. We were all tired. My mom and dad went to lay down for a nap in their room, my brother went to his room to play Xbox, and I went to my room to read. Eventually I must have dozed off.

My bedroom still didn't have a door yet. There was no warning creak of a door closing and the carpet muffled his footsteps. I was startled awake by his heavy hand pulling back the covers and the scruff of his stubble against my thighs.

I clenched my body tight. I still didn't have the strength in my spirit to fight him, but for the first time I resisted. I could feel him beginning to get frustrated. I knew that if I continued to deny him, I would be in for a difficult week. The abuse may happen behind closed doors, but punishment didn't have to.

I heard my brother's bedroom door open. My dad quickly stood up and left my room to try to make the situation look natural, as my brother passed my room to enter the kitchen. I could hear the quiet rumble of my dad's voice making small talk with my brother. I knew this was my chance. I jumped out of bed and quickly went into the bathroom.

When I came out a few minutes later, my dad was sitting in the dining room at the family computer. I avoided eye contact as he smirked "have a good nap?" I only nodded as I headed out the door.

At church that evening I watched as my dad shook hands with church members and lead the choir in songs of worship and wondered what they would all think if they knew what those same hands had done only hours before.

Chapter 12

It is a unique circumstance being hurt by a parent.

If a stranger hurt you, or a best friend violates your trust, if a lover annihilates your self-worth, you can hate them. You can lash out, fight back, or erase them from your life, no matter how difficult that may seem.

But, when your perpetrator is one of the very people who brought you into this world, who make up who you are, and are supposed to provide the safety net for your life are the ones tearing holes through that very net. There is no relief.

You can hate them, but then you will find them reflected in your soul. You can try to cut them from your life, but in the mirror and in your children, there they are. But more than that, you will feel their absence every day for the rest of your life. No matter how deep the hurt lies, the longing and yearning for the love lies even deeper

You can forgive, but despite what they may say, you can never forget. There is no right answer. So, your life becomes a constant balancing act; the rickety bridge across the jungle cavern from the animated movies of our childhood. You enjoy the beauty of the jungle around you, but you never take the next step for granted. The jungle at first glance is lush and green. It is buzzing with life, full and vibrant with beautiful colors and a symphony of birds. However, hiding beneath all that beauty, in the darkest corners behind the tallest trees and the thickest brush, are countless predators and dangers of all sizes and shapes, waiting for your next misstep.

Chapter 13

Saturday night, Levi called to tell me goodnight, just like he did every night. However, this night it was later than what my parents allowed. So, I hid inside the laundry room closet to have our frantic and whispered conversation. I couldn't go to my bedroom because I didn't have a bedroom door. The house had just been remodeled and my room recently added on. The landlord had promised we would have a door for my bedroom to match the rest of the doors shortly after moving in, that had been three weeks ago.

I knew my dad would be furious about this secret phone call for several reasons. Firstly, Levi and I had already spent most of the day together. My parents were the youth directors of our church and had organized a car wash for the teens to earn money for church camp the following week. Afterwards, my mom had allowed me to invite Levi back to the house where a few families from the church had gathered for a cookout. And of course, we would see each other the next morning at church. Secondly, I was breaking dad's rules. The rules were the rules and worse than simply breaking them was trying to hide that you were breaking them. Even worse than *that* was sneaking around and breaking the rules for a *boy*.

Under normal circumstances, Levi would not have called. He wouldn't have risked me getting in trouble, or more importantly, he wouldn't have risked the forthcoming punishment which would have halted communications between us for a whole week. However, what our conversation consisted of that evening made a phone call essential.

Levi and I had only been dating a few months. Well, what counted as dating under my dad's ever-changing rules of proper Christianity. Touching of any kind was forbidden. No hugging, no hand holding, no kissing. But Levi, even at our young age, was perceptive enough to notice that there was more going on than just my reluctance or fear of breaking the rules.

To know me then was to know a very fearful, fragile, tiny girl. During the car wash, something happened between my dad and I that set off alarm bells for Levi. While using the water hose to spray cars, my dad intentionally sprayed me. And not in that normal parent, child playful sort of way. It was a strangely, tense moment that left everyone present with a lingering feeling of awkwardness. Especially me.

As a young girl growing up in a purity culture and being at a church function with all my peers, having my clothes soaked and clinging to my body, left me feeling very exposed. It was clear by the look on my face that I was incredibly embarrassed. I did not like being the center of attention, I hated being singled out. I felt like the punchline of a very cruel joke.

As everyone hurried back to the job at hand, I tried to rush to the restroom to hide the tears in my eyes and tried to dry off with the paper towels the bathroom had to offer. As I came back outside, Levi was waiting by the door with a towel. He said in a low tense voice, "I am very young, I get that." "But I know I love you and I know something isn't right." "Who is hurting you?" I very softly murmured, "My Dad." Levi looked at me with disbelief. I told him to come to the house and I would explain everything. As the echoes of laughter drifted around us, I bared my soul to this fourteen-year-old boy. I told him how my dad had been molesting me since I was ten years old.

Levi was more than a boyfriend to me. We were best friends. We were each other's buoy in a stormy sea. Levi was a big boy, even at fourteen he was 6'4 and clocked in around two hundred pounds. I could see his jaw tensing and hands clinching into fists. Angry was not even close to what he was feeling. I knew I had to get him off the property and away from where my dad was. I put my small hands on his chest and pushed. With a shaky voice I told him, "You have to go."

The phone call that night was for Levi to tell me that he was going to get me help. He was getting me out. Levi was going to tell. I was sick all over. I begged him not to thinking 'What have I done? What would happen now?' I whispered, "I love you" and hung up amid the conversation in fear of being caught. As I crawled out from under the dirty clothes in the closet, I heard my dad yell from the living room "If you don't get with the rules, heads are gonna roll." Boy was he ever right. Although, I don't think he could have ever imagined how true that was. The next day, our world as we knew it completely imploded.

Chapter 14

The next day started as usual for a Sunday morning. I was up early to get ready for church. I would call Levi every Sunday morning to wake him up. First thing he told me was, "I told Mike. He is going to help you."

Mike and Carol were members of our church. Mike was a firefighter and Carol was a dialysis nurse. They weren't the youth leaders, which was my parents. However, they chaperoned a lot of the activities and everyone in the church loved them.

Mike was like a cool uncle. He made us follow the rules, but he also led the charge on shenanigans. I would find out later that Mike had some suspicions that something was amiss in my life before Levi had even reached out to him.

Due to Mike's training, he was well versed in the red flags that indicate abuse; my behaviors and health issues being mine. His position in our community also made him a mandatory reporter. So, when Levi called him late Saturday night, everything fell into place.

Mike reached out to Paul and Emily, the pastor and wife of our church. Paul and Emily were also more than that, our families had been close since we attended the same church back in Missouri. I babysat and cared for their adopted girls since they had been placed with them at the ages of two and three. They were my parent's best friends, but they also loved me dearly.

I'm not sure what the conversations in these two separate households sounded like that night. I can imagine both tears and disbelief. I will never know the well of strength these four humans pulled from, how they kept smiling, "business as usual" faces. How they taught Sunday school classes and hugged the hurting, all the while not being able to reach out to me, a young girl that both couples considered like a daughter. How Mike and Paul were able to shake Stan's hand and discuss the business of the day, as if the entire world had not upended itself, I do not know. How do you wrap your mind and heart around your best friend, business partner, and brother in Christ committing these acts, especially against his own child?

The Sunday service proceeded. After the service, I wanted to walk to the ice cream parlor for lunch with my friends. My dad said no. I was frustrated because I had met all the requirements. Yes, Levi would be there, but so would several others. We also would be outside, not behind closed doors and I had my own money from babysitting. In my mind, there was no reason to deny me this small outing except for their need to have me babysit my brother so they could go out to lunch, just the two of them.

At some point, Bobby came to my room and said Emily was here to get me. I was confused. I came to the door and she said, "come with me, let's go for a ride." I made a small fuss over leaving my brother because that was the whole reason I was stuck at home in the first place. Emily assured me; Paul would take Bobby.

Emily began to back out of the drive, I noticed her eyes brimming with tears. I tried to ignore the pit in my stomach, as she murmured a strangled "Why? "Did you not trust me?" I could only whisper "it's not your fault, I didn't trust anyone." Emily immediately apologized for the selfishness of these questions. She begged for forgiveness for being so blinded she couldn't see what was right in front of her. She then filled me in on what was happening. Paul was confronting my parents and I was going to Mike and Carol's, where I would be safe. A part of my heart began to soar with the possibility of escape from the exhausting terror of the past six years. My mind began to quickly calculate how much trouble I would be in and what fresh hell the consequences would bring.

Someone made sure Levi was there waiting on me. I couldn't stop crying and shivering, even as I curled up next to Levi on Carol's huge, overstuffed sectional.

I held my breath to wait for what would happen next.

Chapter 15

Everyone called him Big Levi. Or Howard if Aunt May had enough of his shenanigans. To me, he was always Levi. He was big, and the oldest sibling in his family, so Big Levi made sense. Levi was quiet until he felt comfortable with you. He was very particular about the way he looked. His hair was always perfectly styled and crispy with gel and the smell of cologne followed him wherever he went.

Levi's home life was pretty rocky at times. He lived with his dad, stepmom, two younger brothers, and a younger sister. But he hadn't always lived with his parents. For most of his childhood, he was raised by his grandpa. This meant that he was close to his aunts and cousins on his dad's side. It was such a foreign concept to me when we started dating. We had lived away from our families since I was ten. But growing up in a tiny village in Ohio, it was pretty common. Everyone was either related to or knew everyone else. Steve and his wife, Mandy, were Levi's best friends and cousins, and you could usually find us at one of three places: their house, the river, or the reservoir.

After Levi's Grandpa died, life changed for Levi. It was so hard for him. He lost a huge part of his identity and felt unmoored and unwanted. He bounced back and forth between parents, but just didn't have a good relationship with his stepdad. So, he settled in the best he could with his dad and stepmom. Levi loved his younger siblings and took their care and protection very seriously. He made a choice that he would always be able to care for himself. And once we started dating and I moved out of my parent's house, he took care of me. He was only fifteen, but he found jobs. There was always a yard to be mowed or raked or some other odd job around town. Steve bought a house and he paid us both to do basic remodeling jobs.

I kept a cooler in my room upstairs at Paul and Emily's. Levi kept my cooler stocked with my favorite snacks and drinks. I never ate much and that always concerned him, so he made sure I always had something close that I would want to eat.

Levi tried to portray himself as big, hard, and tough. But he had the biggest heart. He loved animals. Especially weird ones. While we dated, his favorite pet was a scorpion; one that may or may not have escaped in his room. Levi knew I was lonely at night after he would go home, so he bought me a gerbil and the whole setup including one of those cages with all the cute little tunnels. It gave me someone to take care of and focus on besides myself.

Levi was also very ornery. He never missed an opportunity to prank someone or pull off some silly shenanigan. He had this mischievous giggle that would melt my heart. You couldn't help but join in. His laugh was contagious.

Levi became friends with my brother to have an excuse to hang around our house and see me. I originally started hanging out with Levi to try to get him and my very shy friend Brooke together. I had no interest in dating. Firstly, it was super complicated and secondly, I had recently broken up with Danny. And that was an extremely difficult, long-distance relationship.

After weeks of building up Brooke's confidence, I received a call from her after school. She said, "I can't date Levi." What? I expected her to say that she just chickened out. But no, her response was even more unexpected. Brooke said Levi was crazy about ME. And that she was giving him my number and I should give him a chance.

Levi called me within 10 minutes of getting off the school bus the next day. I told him he was crazy. My dad's rules made dating me impossible and definitely not fun. My brother always had to be around, we couldn't hold hands, it was just so far from a normal teenage romance. Levi didn't care. I laughed, the first of many in our relationship. He always made me laugh, no matter how dark of a place I was in. I told him I would give him a month. For the next two and a half years we dated. He would ask me at the end of every month if he could have one more month.

There was a lot of really hard things that Levi and I went through before, during and after our relationship. But for two and a half years we had a lot of fun and loved each other as much as two kids could ever love each other.

Levi loved being outside. He loved fishing and walking the river. After I moved out, rules were a little more relaxed. At least there was a lot more room to breathe within them. Even after I was out from under my dad's roof, I had a tough time with breaking his rules.

When most teenagers would run wild with the freedom, I still only dipped my toe in.

However, Levi and I did have a lot more alone time together.

We usually spent that time walking from one side of town to the other. Literally. One of my dad's weird rules was that we could be alone if we were walking. So, we did. We held hands until we heard or saw a car coming. That's not to insinuate we didn't find ways to get into some shenanigans. We did.

I had never GIVEN my intimate self to anyone beyond a few stolen kisses. Levi made me feel safe. He protected me and made sure I knew he would never hurt me. He was the first person to ever call me beautiful. Being with him was the first time I felt beautiful. In my 16- -year-old mind, he was my forever. On my 16th birthday, I gave my virginity to Levi. It was different from what I felt when my dad stole my choice from me. This didn't feel like a violation, but a gift to someone who loved and cherished me. This felt safe and exciting. This felt like love.

Levi was always by my side through this journey. He was my hero. I began to call him my Superman. And if he wasn't at school and I wasn't at some appointment for counseling or some other case-related meeting, we were together. If we couldn't be together physically, we were on the phone with each other.

We were usually at the river. I remember one day we had walked miles in the riverbed. The depth of the water ranged anywhere from my ankles to my knees. We had a blast. Splashing and giggling. Suddenly, Levi noticed weird winding tracks in the sand bed. He was convinced it was a snake. "Out. Of. The. Water." Levi sternly ordered speaking the words as they were each their own sentence. I scrambled up the bank and out of the water, scaring a beaver, which was much scarier than the unseen snake. After walking quite a distance down river, we found the offending track maker. It was a MUSSEL! I laughed so hard. I fell backwards into the water. This was a reminder of how Levi always looked out for me.

Levi and I broke up close to my 18th birthday. It had been a long, wonderful, and hard two and a half years. We had many difficulties. By this time, I was in foster care and we were almost two hours apart. It just wasn't fair to him. I wanted him to enjoy his senior year, not spend it chasing me wherever life took me. And we were falling apart. We argued a lot. We were both tired.

My last phone call with Levi was in December of 2003. Since we had broken up, Danny and I had reconnected. I was going to marry Danny and move to Missouri. For me it was the easiest and quickest way out of Ohio.

I called Levi to tell him the news. It just felt fair for him to hear it from me and not the gossip around town. I also called to tell him Stan had finally been incarcerated. I thanked him for all he had been for me. I told him I would always carry part of him with me. Because he saved my life. We cried together. Levi told me he loved me and he told me he would never stop loving me. As much as I wanted to deny his feelings, I knew they were true. I still loved him, but my need to escape was greater than my love in that moment.

In September of 2004 I was married and living back in Indiana when I received an odd call from Paul. It was late at night, around 10 p.m. Paul asked if I had someone with me. I said yes, Danny was there. Paul told me to sit down, he needed to tell me something. Late that evening on a back country road there had been an unbelievably bad car accident. Levi had been detasseling corn all day. The driver of the car Levi was in had been drinking.

Others in the car said Levi told him to slow down or he was going to punch him in the head. Which is very believable and a very Levi thing to say. The driver didn't slow down though. Instead, the car missed a curve on the country road and flipped over, killing Levi instantly.

Even though we had been apart for over a year, I felt like my heart had been ripped from my chest. Despite being married, there was no question, I was going to Ohio. I left the next morning and drove the three hours back to say goodbye, in exactly the first place we said hello.

Levi's family welcomed me back with open arms, like I had never left. They had pictures of Levi's life set up around the church. Even though we had only been together for two of his seventeen years, I was in many of those pictures. His dad said, "It was because Levi didn't smile before you." His dad handed me a notebook that they had found in Levi's room. It was full of letters to me, sketches of the roses that used to paper my walls, that he only drew for me. Lyrics from songs from his favorite bands about undying love. All dedicated to me.

I walked to the front of the sanctuary where he laid in a casket. Hair perfectly crispy, in his signature black jeans. For the first time ever, he looked small.

No one came forward. I think they understood my need to be alone with him. I imagined everything he could have been, the life he should have had. The children he wanted. The chance he would never have to get out of town and have a life of his own.

I thanked him for loving me. For saving me. And then I quietly got to my feet, kissed his cold forehead, and whispered one last "I love you."

I still wonder every day, even in this other lifetime of mine, even though I am married to someone I love with my whole heart and have a son of my own. I wonder what Levi would have been.

Whoever that was, I know he would have been extraordinary.

Chapter 16

Once arriving at Carol and Mike's house, I cried for an awfully long time. I was told my mom was on her way. While waiting for her arrival, I fell asleep with my head in Levi's lap.

I wish I could say that I felt relief, that I felt that help, comfort, and guidance was on its way, the proverbial cool hand on a fevered forehead kind of solace. However, I did not. I felt dread. I knew in my heart there was no separating my parents. My mom had shown me in a thousand tiny ways throughout my life that my dad always came first. My mom would always choose my dad. I knew that in my heart, even as my mind longed for a different outcome.

I watched Emily's van pull down the long gravel driveway.

My mom got out of the van and as soon as she saw me standing on the porch, she collapsed to the ground hysterically sobbing and wailing. She didn't get up to come to me. She didn't run to wrap me in her arms.

I calmly went out to meet her on the lawn and sat down quietly in front of her. I knew I had to remain the calm one, in the wake of her raging emotional ocean. One of us had to be reasonable. It was silly of me to think it would ever be anyone other than me. The louder she wailed, the quieter I spoke. I refused to be drawn into her performance. I told her I was sorry, that I did not know what else to do, that I couldn't go on like that anymore. My mom just kept wailing. She kept asking me what I wanted her to do? Did I want her to leave him? She begged me to tell her what to do. My mother never said she was sorry. She never said she did not know what had been happening. My mother never said she would take care of me, or protect me, or that I would never have to worry about my father hurting me again. My mother never raged that she would kill the man that hurt her child. There was no fierce mother bear suddenly emerging from its cave. There was no lift the car to save my child type of strength. Just wailing sobs of what was she going to do. What did I want her to do? I finally answered with, "whatever is best for you and Bobby." I don't know how long we stayed on the grass. At some point, Mike came and helped my mom back into the van. I walked back inside alone. Emily took my mom home, and while she was there, she gathered some pajamas and clean clothes from my room.

Emily came back and picked me up from Carol and Mike's house, she said I was going home with her and her family for a while. Emily said she didn't know what the next few days, or weeks, or even months looked like for me, but she would be by my side and assured me that I could stay in their home as long as I needed.

Our youth group was already scheduled to leave for church camp the next day. My parents decided, that with everything going on, they needed time alone to figure things out. So, on Sunday, I confessed my dad was molesting me and instead of taking me away and sheltering me or providing comfort and solace to me, my mom agreed with my dad that sending my brother and I away to camp for the next week was "for the best." When I came home at the end of the week, I would be living with Paul and Emily and my father would continue living with my mom and brother in our family's home.

Chapter 17

Dearest Little Alice,

I see you; I know life has not been fair to you. I know you have been silenced for many years, crying out and asking for someone, anyone to help. I see you. For years, I have tried to hold your hand, hug you and it seems I cannot quite grasp you. I stand before you today a man of integrity, a man of honesty, a man that believes that to truly help you, I must advocate for you.

Over the past few years, I see glimpses of you, I can see your sad dark eyes, your heart in shards laying at your feet. I want you to know that I will correct what has been done to you. Alice is working on telling your story because only she knows what you have been through. However, I know enough, and I promise you as a man, I will speak your truth. I will combat those that have done you wrong. It might not make sense to outsiders; however, I will give up everything to ensure you are at peace. I want you to know that I will not forget you. I will let the world burn all around me before I let your memory die.

Once your voice is heard and those who have done you wrong are reprimanded and you at last are sleeping, calmly, safely, and with a full heart, I will say goodbye. I will always be here through the months, years, and decades. Even then, if I am needed, I will forever and always be here for you. I will be the man to lay my hand on your back while you are safely sleeping. I will be the man to rock you when its dark and the doorknob turns. I will be the man with my two hands ready to battle for you. I see you and will never forget you.

Sincerely,
Grant

Chapter 18

Church camp is its own mine field of anxiety for someone like me. But, that particular year, the week of camp was pure hell. I am not sure why my parents, or Paul and Emily, the four adults in charge of my life at the time, thought that sending my brother and I to camp was a good idea, but that's what they did. I'm sure they thought I would be fine and it would give them a chance to figure things out. Levi came too.

At church camp, boys and girls are separated. All I wanted was to sit and hold Levi's hand, like a ship clinging to an anchor in a storm. There was one lady from another church who had very stern words for us after catching us holding hands twice. Of course, there were a lot of ladies from church at camp, but I felt that "church lady" had it out for me during the whole week. She could have never known what had happened the weekend before and only had our best interests and the rules of camp in mind. However, I spent the week angry and annoyed at her.

Also at church camp, there is a meticulous schedule of activities.

I hate playing sports under very normal circumstances. I was small, uncoordinated, clumsy, and without a competitive bone in my body. My life had just come unhinged twenty-four hours previously. The last thing I cared about was kickball. I hate kickball. No, I loathe kickball. I have since the second grade. I didn't like being put on the spot to be a kicker or a pitcher. I didn't like standing in the field waiting for the big, red, rubber balls to fly at my face. The thick glasses I have worn since kindergarten don't really pair well with kickball either. I have short arms and legs. I can't run. I can't pitch. I can't catch. I did not want to play kickball.

I also couldn't eat. I had struggled with stomach complications for a long time. This was one of the major health issues that had concerned Mike. I dealt with intense and constant nausea on a regular basis. So, of course, with the stress of recent events these problems were very prevalent that week.

Oddly enough, the only thing I could stomach was pizza combos. I had no money for the snack bar but my friend Brooke, and of course Levi, kept supplying me with combos and Mountain Dew.

Finally, by Wednesday, Paul and Emily returned and explained my situation to "Church Lady." So, Thursday and Friday were finally peaceful. I still wasn't allowed much time with Levi; however, I was allowed to sit out kickball and stay in the cabin and sleep, which was all I really wanted to do anyway.

Emily pulled me aside late Wednesday night for a heart to heart. We spoke about how long it had been going on and why I hadn't come forward. How could she support me and what the trip home would entail? Paul, Emily, Mike, and Carol had decided to contact the authorities. As a firefighter, a nurse, and pastor, they were all mandatory reporters and they all took that seriously. I am so thankful that they did.

It was quite common in these type of situations for the "Church" to handle this type of problem within the congregation. What that would often mean is that there would be no outside knowledge or intervention. The church would require some type of confession in front of the congregation. I was later told that Stan had done this. I do not know and can't imagine what he said or how the members of the church received it. Then, we would have some type of intense family and individual counseling by the pastor and his wife. In something this severe, they may even suggest some type of rehabilitation retreat for the offender. But they definitely would have done everything in their power to keep the issue in the church and the family whole with no legal repercussions for the offender. In the case of my father and I, the adults that Levi and I confided in chose to follow the steps needed to protect me at all costs by reporting the abuse to the proper authorities.

On Friday, we headed back to Ohio from Kentucky. Halfway home, we stopped at a park, where Mike and Carol met us. While the other kids and teens stretched their legs and ran around, my brother and I loaded up into Emily's van. While the rest of the group went home with Mike and Carol, Emily and Paul drove us to a neighboring town from where we lived in Ohio to be interviewed for the first time by Social Workers at the Department of Children's Services (DCS).

I suppose that isn't entirely true. About a year or so before, we had been interviewed by DCS. I am not sure who reported it at the time. Our electricity had been disconnected the previous winter. The electric bill had become so high that my parents decided it would have to wait until they received their tax refund to catch up on payments and get it reconnected. My dad's grand solution was to run a series of industrial extension cords to the landlord's house that was about five hundred feet or so in front of our house. We could power one item at a time, we had a kerosene heater, and a gas stove.

That time, my parents took us to DCS. The caseworker asked us routine questions about our living situation, discipline methods, and schooling arrangements because we were homeschooled, or what counted as schooling with my parents. I remember thinking that if the case worker had asked the right questions or if she had spoken to me alone without my brother, I would have told her and reached out for help then. However, she hadn't.

The people of the church came together with a love offering and paid the bill in full and life in our household continued. I wonder if Stan was nervous that day? Was he worried that with just a few words his secret would be out? Or did he know the control he had over me? Did he know that the fear of his consequences suffocated my instinct to save myself?

Chapter 19

After Levi and I told my secret, there was a lot of turmoil in every part of my life, but mostly in my living arrangements. The first place I lived at was with Paul and Emily who had three kids of their own at this time. The two girls they adopted who were five and six, and a new infant who was about eight months old. Just as I was the go- to caretaker for the older girls, I had been helping Emily with the baby since she was born. So not only were our families together a lot, but I was also a constant figure in their home.

I am not sure how the decision came about for me to stay at their home; my choice at the time would have been to stay at Carol and Mike's. They had a much quieter home life and were very nurturing with me. But at the time their work schedule would have left me alone a lot and I don't think my parents were comfortable with that. I would like to think it was because of some deep concern for my well-being, but more than likely it was more about behavior monitoring and control.

With three kids of their own and a church to manage, and now a public nightmare unfolding in their congregation, their plate was overflowing. Still, they welcomed me into their home. They cleaned out a room in the second story so that I would have privacy and my own space. Emily and Paul explained to me that there were house rules to follow along with whatever boundaries my parents put into place, but that they weren't my parents and weren't trying to raise me.

It wasn't like foster care, but it wasn't freedom either. I was always welcome to be included in their family meals and activities, however I always felt separate at the same time.

For the first few months after the secret came out, we didn't visit or contact our family in Indiana, although we lived closer to them than we had in years. No one outside of the circle of people involved knew what was happening. An article ran in the local paper with no identification, of course. It didn't need to identify us; where we lived was a tiny village. People put the pieces together on their own.

Keeping this from our extended family was my parents' highest priority, so that was why I lived with Paul and Emily instead of my aunts or grandparents. Our family eventually found out of course, but that wasn't until much later.

After returning from church camp, I went to my parents' house while my dad was at work. By this time there was already a "No Contact Order" put in place by DCS. I gathered up as many of my things as I could to make my new room at Paul and Emily's feel like home. As I was packing my belongings, I could tell my room had been searched through. My bookcase was out of order. I recalled a few days earlier my mom calling and asking me where my diary was. I had always kept several journals. One journal kept the details of my day-to-day life, one was full of stories I had written, and another held the letters I wrote to the Lord. All of them were very closely held. All of them hidden away. I remembered her asking where they were kept. When I asked her why she replied that she needed to get rid of them in case the detectives searched our house. My dad would be turning himself into the authorities and they were afraid that would lead to a search of my room and personal items. I had always kept these journals in regular spiral notebooks that were hidden in plain sight among the books in my bookcase.

My bedroom has always been a very sacred place to me. I kept it clean and organized. I spent my own money from babysitting to decorate it. Everything was leopard print and matching. I collected miniature purses with their matching high heeled shoes. Pictures I had made from my scrapbooking supplies and favorite quotes, as well as snapshots of Levi and my friends scattered the walls. It was cute and it was mine.

Over the years I had become numb to the nightly violation. This time was different. In part because this betrayal was led by my mom. It felt like they had walked right into the depths of my heart and trampled mud everywhere.

I knew there wasn't a lot of time to get my things packed and ready, so as became routine in this time of my life, I took a deep breath, wiped my eyes, and packed up my belongings. I felt so many things in that moment. Anger, fear, and sadness.

When I got my things back to my new room at Emily and Paul's, I spent the evening making the space my own. I tried to go about settling into some kind of normalcy.

Emily was my main pillar of comfort and support. She was always available to me. She would let me talk, scream, and cry. No matter what I needed, she was there. Emily and Paul also acted as mediators between my parents and me. My mom could come around or call anytime, she just did not. My dad had already lost a huge part of the control he had over me so he tried every way possible to keep what power he had by sending messages through my mom and even setting up an after-church meeting, despite the no-contact order in place. The meeting was set up for after church one Sunday. Levi, myself, Mom, Dad, Emily, and Paul all met in Paul's office at the church. I remember Emily's saying afterward that she had never understood why people would say someone looked green when they felt sick until she saw my face in that moment. My dad had everything ready for this meeting and prepared with scripture to back up all his arguments.

One thing to understand about my father is that he is a master of words. He knew how to use them as a weapon and a trap. My dad had a way of winding your words in and out, up, and down, until you didn't even remember the point you were trying to make. I had known the night before that the meeting had been arranged, so I was prepared. Or as prepared as I could be. I had one thing to say. I was going to say it no matter what.

My dad started off demanding forgiveness. I glanced at the others in the room, did they hear him too? I felt as if I had walked in on a tv show during a commercial break. Had I missed something? Where was the apology, the repentance that he so loved to preach about? Did it happen before I came in? It couldn't have. I was the first one in the office. For the next thirty minutes I listened patiently as he spoke on and on. My dad explained to me that by withholding forgiveness from the sinner, I became just as guilty *as* the sinner. That in the eyes of God, "sin was sin." No sin worse than the other. As I listened, rage filled my chest like lava. But I held my tongue. I knew if I got roped into an argument the one thing I wanted to say would lose its impact. I waited until he had said his peace and sat back, smug smile, arms crossed against his chest. I took a deep breath.

In my mind the words came out as a lion's roar, but in reality, they came out just above a whisper. "You no longer get to speak to me as my parent. You have forfeited the right to be my father. Someday, maybe we can be friends, but you will *never* again be my dad." I didn't wait for a response. I stood and walked out of the office and ran to the parsonage.

Emily caught up to me and ushered me into her bedroom where I collapsed on the floor. I was hyperventilating. I could not cry. There were no tears. Emily quietly said "Scream." I looked at her like she had two heads. She repeated "Scream, Paul has the girls. It's just us. Scream as loud as you can." So, I did. Until my voice was gone and my throat sore. And finally, the tears came.

Chapter 20

Emily found a counselor for me through another Baptist church in a town about 30 minutes from where we lived. The drive up there was incredibly quiet. I really had no idea what to expect. The church itself was a huge building. Walking into an empty church is such an awkward feeling. When I was younger, I remember a preacher saying he always kept the church doors open, in case someone ever needed to come into a safe space. Figuratively and literally, I suppose. I never felt as if I was walking into a sanctuary when I came into an empty church. It just felt like trespassing. Like Belle sneaking into the West Wing.

I finally found my way to the office and sat nervously in the waiting area. My life felt like a constant waiting room. I was always waiting. I was waiting to repeat my story, waiting for answers and consequences of telling my story, waiting for my mom, waiting for it all to be over. There were just so many loose ends. I was caught in a giant web and it felt like everyone had a direction but me.

I was not thrilled to be meeting with a counselor. I did not want solutions. I wanted to be heard and seen. I did not want explanations. I wanted to see the anger I felt towards my parents reflected in the eyes of an adult. I wanted someone to be on my side. I wanted to feel like my anger and sadness were valid.

There was no discussion about finding and meeting with a counselor. It was just done. So, I went. I sat down at a long conference table and was given a clipboard of paperwork to fill out. There was no one beside me, just tiny 16-year-old me at a huge table. I remember looking at the questionnaire in front of me. The first question was "Why are you seeking our services?"

I wanted to scream. I wanted to break the pencil in half. Didn't someone tell them why I was here? Surely there was a better way to introduce themselves to my situation than for me to have to write the details out again, to another stranger.

But being the good girl that I always tried to be, I didn't even roll my eyes. I just started to write the answers to the question:

I was sexually abused by my father since I was 10 years old. I recently told my boyfriend, who told the authorities. I have anxiety.

The counselor came to collect me. I don't remember her name. She was not a psychiatrist or a psychologist. She was a pastor's wife. She was very petite and mousy. Her voice was quiet when she said "Well, let's talk about your anxiety…."

I sat for 45 minutes and listened to how the Lord does not want us to be afraid or anxious. I listened to her tell me that the Lord doesn't cause things like this in our lives, but sometimes He *allows* these things for His greater purpose.

At first, I nodded knowingly, but as she continued speaking to me, and reading verses from the Bible, my brain caught up. Sometimes it felt like two people inside my brain. One that ran on autopilot and went through the acceptable motions and behaving as expected. Then there was the part of my brain that was raging and incredulous.

I lived through this hell either to teach me a lesson or so I could be a lesson. What kind of sense does that make? I did not want to be a lesson.

I did not want to be taught how to be a lesson. I wanted a hug. I wanted an adult to tell me that I was not a bad girl. That this was not my fault. I wanted someone to teach me how to take all these broken pieces of my soul and make something resembling a whole person again. I did not need words and instructions from hundreds of years ago, I didn't need an ethereal being, or the image of someone carrying me down the beach of life. I needed a real person. I needed to be held and loved.

This counselor was just another person that ignored and overlooked the storm raging in my life. There was not a single person that acknowledged the actual root of what my problems were. No one wanted to address why I was there. In their office or in their home.

I went back to my temporary bedroom with a pamphlet about trusting Jesus to take my burden and a few chapters in Psalms to read. This was what was considered "getting me help" for years of sexual abuse at the hands of my own father. I attended these sessions quietly and obediently every week for about a month. At that point, my mom took over driving me to these appointments. My mom pointedly asked me if I felt like these sessions were really working? Did I feel like they were worth the time and drive? I knew what she was implying.

They weren't working. They were not a solution. But they did feel like a Band-Aid. Even though we didn't address the real issues or come up with any real solutions, she did sit and listen to only me for 45 minutes a week. We didn't talk about what hurt, but for 45 minutes a week, I felt important.

But I understood where my mom was going with her questions. It was an inconvenience to take almost three hours out of her day off to drive me there, wait for me, then drive back. So, I just stopped going and once again I was on my own.

Chapter 21

I never had an expectation of what would happen after I told my secret. There was never a thought or plan to ever tell someone. My father had always told me that by telling I would ruin my family. My mom would leave, his career in the church would be destroyed, everything would be over. I did not want to cause that. So, I knew I would never, ever tell. There was no planning behind telling Levi, it just happened. The night before the secret was out, I let myself imagine what the next day would look like.

I expected the world to stop. It didn't. I expected my mom to sweep me up in her arms and save me from the bad guy. She did not. These were distorted perceptions of protection.

Instead, life continued. While I was disintegrating inside, I was expected to continue with the daily tasks of normal life and keeping up with appearances. I thought that by telling, a burden would be lifted and the secrecy, lies, and hiding would be over. Instead, they became a continued way of life.

This new life became a maze I had to navigate on my own. My mom reminded me often that she just "wanted her life back." Due to the recent events, she had to get a full-time job, as well as deal with the family's fall from grace. She was no longer a respected lady in the church that others looked up to. She lost her best friend because I now lived with her. It is hard to avoid visiting your daughter when she lives with the person you used to hang out with the most.

My brother was angry. He felt that I was always the center of everyone's attention. He felt I always got anything I wanted, because my mom bought me things to soothe her guilt for not being there for me. My mom didn't spend time with me. She didn't visit or talk to me on the phone. But each day when Levi got home from school, he and I would walk to the Dollar Store where my mom worked. I would walk around the store picking out snacks and she would pay for them at the end of her shift.

Paul and Emily did the best they could. They were in no place to have a teenager dropped in the middle of their lives. Especially a teenager as broken as I was.

In my heart, I felt like nothing more than an inconvenience. A problem to throw lackluster solutions at. Except, no one wanted to face the real problem. Just the symptoms and the behaviors. No one held the person who was actually guilty accountable. So, my belief was that it must be my fault. I wreaked all this havoc on everyone's life. No one told me it was my fault, but no one told me it was not.

This was not a new feeling to me. I had felt like I had been in the way my whole life. Throughout my whole childhood I had felt like an afterthought unless I could use my maturity, intelligence, or talent to shine a positive light on my parents or the church.

These times of trauma were no different. I wonder if either of my parents ever stopped and took a moment to put themselves in my shoes. I remember in the early days thinking about all the ways everyone's lives had to change. I felt like everyone considered my reporting of the abuse more of the catalyst for that change than the acts of abuse were.

One night my mom came to stay with me because Emily and Paul were out of town. Early that morning she had taken Stan into the sheriff's department to "turn himself in."

They had gone early in the morning so that he would be seen by the judge that day and not have to stay overnight in the county jail. I can recall so vividly sitting in the living room at Emily and Paul's house. There was a big picture window, the sun had gone down a while ago. Neither one of us had turned on the light. It was just my mom and me dimly lit by the security lamp outside. Mom told me every detail of the day. How she was interviewed, but not what she said. How they took my dad back to be questioned. She said she waited in the lobby for a long time. As she was looking out the window, she saw a line of inmates in shackles and handcuffs, with my dad bringing up the end of the line, as they were loaded in a van to go to the courthouse to be seen by the judge. My dad got lucky. By being there early, he was able to see the judge that day. My dad was released on his own recognizance, meaning he promised he would show up for court and be a good guy in the meantime. Since he had no prior history, the judge released him instead of holding him until trial or setting a bond amount.

I remember feeling so sad and heartbroken as my mom sobbed. It all felt like my fault. I immediately picked up the clunky house phone and dialed my own home phone number. When my dad picked up, I sobbed out how sorry I was that he went through that. I even told him I forgave him. My dad told me that it was okay. That he forgave me too.

Can you imagine? This was the manipulation that was rampant throughout my whole life. The tension of feeling like the inconvenient child. Always in the way. Always causing drama and stirring up strife. If something went wrong, the narrative always became twisted so that the blame fell squarely on me. Again, no one ever told me it was my fault, but no one told me it was not. Actions speak louder than words.

This type of manipulation is prevalent among abusers, especially in faith based, fundamentalist communities. The child, who has already been victimized, is then pressured to quickly forgive, and put the abuse behind them. It is instilled in them the importance of saving the reputation of the abuser.

I was strongly admonished by the elder Christians in our church, to "have grace, as Jesus did." I was repeatedly reminded of Jesus' crucifixion and how, even as sinful as we were as people, Jesus died and extended grace to us. One little old lady at church one morning pulled me into a tight hug and whispered in my ear "Sometimes, Daddies just love their little girls too much."

There were so many adults that put the responsibility on my shoulders to make things right. To pack up the years of abuse in a box and sit it up on the shelves of my mind. To excuse the choices my father had made.

My father and others were quick to provide me with verses such as Luke 17:3-4: *"Take heed to yourselves: if thy brother trespass against thee rebuke him; and if he repents, forgive him."* Oddly enough no one backed up just one verse to Luke 17:2 where Jesus said, *"It were better for him that a millstone were hanged about his neck, and he cast into the sea, than that he should offend one of these little ones."*

This was Jesus, himself, telling his disciples the importance of protecting *"these little ones."* There is no need for educated translations to know who these little ones are.

It felt like it was all my fault. It felt like it was my job to fix it. No one took the time to tell me it wasn't.

Chapter 22

My mom picked me up from Paul and Emily's for a rare afternoon together. We went through the drive-thru at a fast-food restaurant and shared lunch in the car. Neither one of us enjoyed being out in public, there was too much to process. We usually sat in the car or at a picnic table when we were together.

I am not sure exactly when this was. It seems like it was autumn or late summer, as it was still ridiculously hot outside.

We drove for a long time. We were going to meet with Stan's attorney. I will let you process the irony.

Mom made this seem like another important, necessary appointment. There were so many at this point; DCS, the sheriff, a counselor. So, meeting with an attorney seemed normal. Of course, looking back, I question how I could have been so stupid. But, I was a child, I was sheltered. I had so many conflicting feelings and ideas. I felt so much guilt and shame. I was manipulated.

Everything was about our family. It did not matter what was best for me, it mattered what was best for the family. Although I was out of his house, I was still very much under his control. Our "family" still followed his lead. I recall being taught the definition of obedience from an early age, "*Do what you are told, when you are told, with the right heart attitude."* So, we did. Stan's goal was to save himself. He sold it under the guise of "keeping his family together." We all acknowledged the legal battle and separation of our family, however no one involved ever addressed the reason all of this had happened. My parents, brother and even members of our church went about life as if all of this were normal. Or even worse, as if these circumstances were a result of my behavior.

So, meeting with my abuser's attorney seemed plausible. Yes, it was told to me, that he was "our" attorney, for our family.

My mother and I sat in two dark leather chairs opposite a wooden desk that took up most of the tight, frigid office. There were floor-to-ceiling bookcases filled with huge three-ring binders and dark covered legal textbooks. I felt swallowed whole. It was hard to hear and harder to speak. It was as though my brain was teeming with bees and my throat blocked by a boulder. I was trembling, uncontrollably.

I must have seemed like such an easy target.

There wasn't a lot said. There didn't need to be. I remember the attorney opening with the fact that he didn't need to hear my side. We didn't need to discuss the truth of the accusations either way. That was not necessary information to him.

What he wanted to know, most importantly was, did I want to see my dad go to prison? Did I want to see him behind bars with real bad guys? With real criminals? At the time, the only picture of prison I had was what you see in movies. It was bad.

Of course, I said no. Again, I want to reiterate, no one had ever expressed to me, let alone impressed upon me, that what had happened to me was an abuse, let alone a crime. I didn't feel like this harm was done *to* me, but instead as though I had somehow been complicit. Since I was made to feel it was partly my fault, I felt I had to be the one to fix it. And Stan's attorney was right there to point me to a solution: "At this time I choose to exercise my right to plead the Fifth Amendment in this matter." Over and over again. "Keep saying it to every question." "You don't have to lie, because you say nothing and then it's over, there is nothing they can do. Don't answer any questions." This was not advice. He could not advise me. Contrary to what my mom had said earlier, he was not my attorney. The attorney made clear his job was not to decide guilt or innocence but to support and guide Stan to the most positive outcome. So, I would have to figure this out alone. Also, I could not discuss this case with anyone, so I was told not to tell anyone I was there. "But what if they forced me to answer?" I asked. "Don't worry, if you plead the fifth, there is nothing they can do. It's over," he said.

"That is what you want, right? Dad not to go to jail and for all of this to be over?" my mom asked. I looked silently between them and the attorney reiterated "so this is the plan, we are going to plead the fifth?"

I glanced at my mom who was crying, her eyes pleading. I took a deep breath. I must save my family, right? With a sickening dread in the pit of my stomach, my chest clogged with held breath, and my brain buzzing with what felt like the sound of TV static, I replied, yes, this is the plan. I will plead the fifth."

Chapter 23

As a young girl, if you had asked me what I wanted to be when I grew up, my answer would have been extraordinary. I don't even know where I learned that word. Nevertheless, that's what I wanted.

While other girls my age were imagining weddings and beauty pageants, I was pretending to run huge companies, or being the lead partner in a huge law firm. My Barbies routinely held trials with Barbie as Judge and, myself represented by Barbie's little sister Skipper. I relished in declaring "Your Honor, I rest my case." Thus, successfully bringing the evil Gaston to justice for his nefarious ways. I wasn't allowed a normal Ken doll, so I had the Beast from the Disney movie, who conveniently played the part of Gaston. Who, of course, unfairly locked Belle away and killed the Beast.

I pictured myself as a doctor, someone who healed the broken and defenseless. Bringing those who hurt others to justice. I spent my childhood pretending and dreaming of a life spent healing and defending those hurt, left out or left behind. Many times, I was told I would have been better suited to the generations of the past who protested injustice.

My dreams were to lead. To be strong, to stand on my own. As a young girl, before the abuse began and withered my confidence and belief in myself, I wanted and believed I could conquer the world.

Although this book may not be a fiery protest, or a speech that brings peace to the world, or a cure to all diseases, maybe my story will bring hope to someone. Maybe knowing they aren't alone, that through hard work, patience, and endurance, their life of pain and suffering can be transformed into a life of joy. If I can reach that one person with my story, my life will have indeed been extraordinary.

Chapter 24

I bounced around quite a bit in the weeks after the implosion of my family's lives. The first place I stayed was with Emily and Paul. I stayed with them until after Christmas. Around January, my parents felt that I lacked the proper supervision a teenage girl needed. My dad especially felt that space needed to be put between Levi and me.

My six-year molestation was revealed to my Nanny and Poppy, my mom's parents in a very startling phone call from my dad's sister in the middle of the night. Stan's sister had found out by word of mouth. My Grandma, Stan's mom had told her that there was nothing more that could be done. She was not taking that for an answer. She wanted me out, no matter how that needed to happen. She looked up my grandparents' number in the phone book and called. My aunt knew that despite the differences between the families over the years, my mom's side of the family would not back down and they would make sure that I was safe.

My mom's sister, Aunt Nancy and her husband, Uncle Bruce came and picked me up and took me back to their home in Indiana. They had their guest room cleaned and organized for me to move in. My uncle Bruce knew music was especially important to me, so he had bought me a hot pink "Teen Bedroom Starter Kit." It had a hot pink CD player, alarm clock, and desk lamp. That was his quiet way of making me feel welcome.

One major change that happened during my stay with my aunt and uncle was I started wearing pants. I had not worn pants since the fourth grade due to our religious beliefs. Nancy took me to the local mall. I filled my arms with every style and color of jeans I could carry and spent an hour in the fitting room trying each one on. I left the store with at least ten new pairs of jeans and the first and biggest smile I had worn in months. It was a small, but substantial step out from under Stan's controlling hand.

I liked staying with my aunt and uncle. I liked being around my other aunts and my grandparents, though I missed Levi incredibly. We talked on the phone nightly. However, nothing eased the ache of not seeing him every day.

My mom kept promising to come and see me on the weekends, she even offered to bring Levi with her. It was a three-hour trip. But she never came. I stayed with my aunt for six weeks and she didn't come once. Each Friday evening, she would call with a different excuse for why she couldn't come that weekend.

We were nearing Levi's birthday in February. I had been doing small jobs around the house to earn money to buy gifts for him. Bruce even took me to the mall to buy Levi a t-shirt from his favorite rock band.

All the adults in my life decided that it would be okay for me to come back to Ohio for the week of his birthday and Valentine's Day. I would be staying with Levi's aunt. In the weeks leading up to the visit, I begged my mom to please not back out. She promised that she would be there to pick me up and bring me home.

The day had come. My bags were packed, my new jeans hidden in the bottom. I was excited to finally be just a few hours away from seeing my mom and hugging Levi. As the hour approached, the anxiety began creeping in. Sure enough, an hour before my mom was set to arrive, the phone rang. She wasn't coming. My aunt was furious with her younger sister. Not because she wanted me to go, but because my mom had let me down yet again. Nancy and Bruce canceled their plans for the day and drove me to Ohio themselves. I was in town for three days before my mom came to see me.

I was only supposed to stay for a week at Levi's aunt's house. However, acting like a teenager for once, I refused to go back. Levi's aunt was a single woman in her twenties and was happy for the company and I didn't want to leave. Staying near Levi these weeks was the extent of my teenage rebellion. Those weeks were fun and happy despite the turmoil. Levi and I spent our evenings and weekends fishing as spring took over the world. But all good things must end. April brought the world crashing back in.

Chapter 25

My parents had made the decision to move out of the little town we lived in when the secret came out. My family moved to a house several counties over along the river. My mom had gotten a job at a dollar store in a nearby town and they had also found a church in the area. It was a clean start with their own narrative of the family tragedy. It really made no difference to me. I had rarely seen my mom and saw my brother even less. However, legally, it did make a difference. When my parents moved from one County to another County, so did our case. It wasn't long before the Department of Child and Family Services began knocking on their new door.

After a flurry of business cards left in the door imploring my parents to return their call, there came an official summons. My parents were subpoenaed.

Nancy and Bruce arrived to pick me up in the middle of the night. They had come to whisk us away. This time my brother would be coming with me.

I was sad and so angry. I was exhausted. I had no idea if the place I woke up in the morning was going to be the same place I laid my head at night. I felt so guilty. None of the people that took me in were in a place to take on this responsibility. I tried extremely hard to be a good house guest. To be polite and grateful and to pull my weight with household chores. I just wanted to have a place to call home. I had been living out of a backpack for months now.

Back to Indiana we went. We settled into a routine back at Nancy's. You know when you are riding in the car during a rainstorm, the rain beats down and drowns out the radio and you can't see through the windshield? Then the car goes under an overpass bridge and for a few very quick seconds, everything is calm and quiet. That's what coming back to my aunt's home felt like. Relief, but I knew it wouldn't last for long. This was the most time my brother and I had spent together in a long time. We didn't talk about what happened or what was going to happen. We just existed together. By this point I was running low on patience. I was running out of smiles and charm. My mask was wearing thin. I slept most of the day and read into the wee hours of the morning.

I was beginning to be angry with God. I still clung to my faith, but the threads were fraying. I couldn't understand how this could be His will or plan for my life. My aunt was becoming concerned with my mental health. I had secretly began cutting again. Always small cuts, hidden away on my thighs and stomach. But the anxiety attacks weren't as easy to hide. I hated leaving the house. I would hide in my room, coming out to sneak snacks after everyone was asleep. However, my father refused to sign guardianship of my brother and I over to Nancy. That meant she couldn't enroll us in school (which I could not have managed anyway), but also, she could not get us any type of medical or mental health treatment. My dad had tied her hands. We were "**HIS** kids." We were stuck in a hamster wheel of grief; never knowing what was coming next.

I didn't know what exactly was going on with my parents back in Ohio. There was still a protection order against my dad, and my mom simply didn't speak to me. I wasn't mad at her yet. I still longed to talk to her. I wanted her comfort. I wanted her to be the strong one, even for a ten-minute phone call. I knew things were tense. I could hear it in my aunt's voice, see it in her eyes. I could never imagine what would happen next.

Mother's Day was coming. I had spent the weeks prior working on a heart shaped shadow box with miniature tin kitchen utensils for mom to hang in her new kitchen. I told myself she would come and see us. She had to. It was Mother's Day. Tensions mounted as the day drew near.

Thursday night before Mother's Day, the phone rang. I could hear my mom's hysterical voice all the way across the room. I waited patiently for my aunt to calm her down and to find out what was happening. It turns out, you don't have to be present at court for the judge to make a decision. My parents had ignored the summons. Several of them actually. When they did finally stand before the judge at the County Family Court, they were ordered to have us at the DFS office by noon the next day. I am not sure what the consequences were, but my mom finally took them seriously.

My aunt and uncle decided we would all pack up in the RV, including my grandparents, and face this head on. As we packed just enough for the weekend, we never even fathomed that Bobby and I would not be returning with the rest of the family. I gently packed away my gift for mom for Mother's Day.

As time was of the essence, we drove straight to the DFS office. It is a brick box in the middle of what seems like a lake of black top. From the outside it is hard to notice the windows and doors. My mom was waiting in the parking lot. She met us at the RV door. This was a rare time when my parents were separated. There were many laws my mom would break, and many consequences she would willingly face to be by my dad's side. However, the wrath of her family was not one.

My mom was already shaking and crying as we climbed down from the RV steps. Whatever was coming, we would face it together. We walked into the building seven people strong. For that one moment I wasn't alone. In that one moment in time, I felt protected. But it didn't last. We walked in as a family. Bobby and I would walk out five hours later as foster kids.

Chapter 26

Walking into the dim, coolness of the DCFS office, I felt the bravado of each adult in my family begin to waiver against the barrier of legalities and red tape. Three case workers approached us, hands raised to waist height, in a classic "we come in peace" gesture. One of the ladies asked my brother and I to follow her into another room while the adults talked. "Everything will be fine. We are just going to fill your family in on what's going on and then we will figure out what happens next." All of this said with huge, clown-like smiles and a high-pitched voice, as if I were seven instead of seventeen. She even asked if we would like to color. I looked at her as if she had grown a second head. "No, thank you. I don't want to color. I want to know what is going on." I was still being polite and minding my manners. It was early in the day. We made small talk as the minute hand on the clock slowly ticked away.

Eventually the case worker separated my brother and me. Since this was a new county, the only information they had was what was gathered by the county we had moved from. So naturally, the caseworkers needed to conduct their own interviews. At this point, my manners began to fade. I had already answered these questions. Many times over. I was done giving statements. I was done answering questions. The tears began to fall, slowly at first, but once the dam began to break, the small office was filled with the sound of my sobs. They were loud, ragged, and ugly. These sobs came from the depths of my soul. I stood up and pushed my chair away from the table and demanded "I want my mom and I want to leave now. Let me out of this room."

The caseworker looked shocked. I was shocked. This was so out of my character. I was loud and belligerent. I was shaking and hysterical. The lady asked me to calm down. "Let me get you a soda and a snack." There was no polite "no thank you" this time. This time I screamed "I DON'T WANT A SNACK; I WANT MY MOM."

The caseworkers continued to reassure me with vague words, promising that I would see my mom soon. I paced the room like a lion in a cage. We had been there for several hours already. My brother was allowed to come back into the room with me. We didn't talk much. There were no windows to see outside. My stomach roiled with anxiety and anger.

The question always arises, why didn't we just return to Indiana with our other family? If protection and distance from our father was the main prerogative, that was definitely covered. To say that my mom's side of the family didn't like Stan was an understatement. It was a well-known fact for most of my life that my grandparents and aunts had never approved of him. If we stayed with them, the no-contact with Stan was an easy fix.

The other major factor in this equation was distance and jurisdiction. Our case was in Ohio, my family lived in Indiana. Now, once again if my parents had been willing to sign over guardianship, even temporarily, all of this could have been avoided. However, my father especially refused to relinquish that control, and my mother simply followed right along.

For us to be able to return to Indiana with our family, several things would need to take place. First, the case and our custody would need to be transferred to Indiana. A case worker would need to be able to visit us at least every 30 days and the state frowns upon long road trips at their expense. But also, we would need a caseworker that could provide us with the support and services we may need throughout the case.

Second, everyone would need background checks as well as a home study. A home study is a fancy name for a safety inspection. Those were also easy tasks to accomplish.

The biggest factors in all these tasks were simply time. Honestly, none of us imagined we would be in foster care for long. We knew nothing about how any of this worked. Foster care and removal was something that happened to bad families. We never dreamed this would be something that any of us would be a part of. We didn't understand how legalities and red tape could drag things along.

My family decided that it wasn't worth pursuing all the requirements for kindred care. In their minds, by the time everyone was approved and all the legal terms were fulfilled, we would be reunited with our mom anyhow.

The protection plan for my mother to follow for us to be returned to her custody was simple:

1. Keep a job
2. Keep a safe home environment
3. Maintain no contact and have no continued relationship with the perpetrator: our father.

Everyone agreed that especially with the added aid and support that our family provided, we should be home by our next court date, which was in just a few weeks.

In my mind, I imagined my family in the other room raging the same type of battle. I didn't realize that my brother and I were in a holding room, passing time until they found a suitable foster home that would take us. My family had left hours ago to head back to Indiana to rally the troops. My mom went home to spend what should have been her last few nights with Stan before our family returned to move her out.

Chapter 27

While our family retreated and regrouped, my brother and I were still in the same office we had been in for the last three or four hours. By now, my anger had run out, my sobs had subsided to quiet little shudders of breath, my head ached, and I was utterly exhausted. The fight had drained out of me like the tide leaves the shore at the end of the day.

Now that we were quiet, our assigned caseworker came in to introduce herself and explain what was happening and what the next steps would be. Her name was Connie, and I despised her. She had thin black hair pulled back with a barrette and the papery dry skin and wrinkles around her mouth of a long-time smoker. Connie could have easily been 36 or 56, no one could tell. But worse of all she was tepid. There were never straight answers when it came to Connie.

Connie sat down with us at the long conference table. I was the picture of an angry teenager. I had my legs pulled up in the chair, hugged tight to my body with my arms crossed around them. I refused to speak or acknowledge her presence. Connie began by apologizing that we had been waiting so long. I let out a sarcastic chuckle. "Where is my mom?" I demanded. This is the point where she informed us that our mother, along with our aunts and grandparents, had been gone for several hours. We had been waiting so long in the office because they were doing their best to find a home that would take both of us together. Our foster mom was on her way and should be there in about twenty minutes.

Connie said that she didn't know how long we would be in foster care, that depended on my mother's ability to accomplish and adhere to the protection plan. This was Friday, we would not be allowed contact with our mom or family members until our scheduled supervised visit. We didn't know exactly how many days that would be, hopefully only a week to ten days.

Connie explained that my aunt had left my overnight bag with her. I was glad that I would have my pajamas and a change of clothes, but I knew that I had only packed enough for an overnight stay in the RV. I didn't have any shampoo or body wash. I had a toothbrush, toothpaste, pajamas, and one change of clean clothes. That wasn't enough for a whole weekend, let alone "as long as it takes for my mom to accomplish and adhere to the protection plan." Connie explained that we would get everything worked out within the next week. The state would provide us with a stipend of money to get us our necessities. For now, we would just have to make do with what we have and to be thankful because most kids don't even have an overnight bag. Again, I rolled my eyes. I turned to Connie and asked "Do you have anything actually helpful to add to this situation? I am not hearing any actual answers to my questions." Connie then informed me that my attitude was not helpful, everyone was doing their best to help us. "I don't want your help. I was perfectly fine where I was, Connie, but thanks." At this point she finally gave up. She said we would talk when I had settled in a little better. My foster mom would be there any moment. So, I turned my back, put my head down on the table and waited.

It was now the end of the day and the office was closing. My bravado having been completely exhausted, I began to be terrified of the idea of spending the night with strangers. My mind began to fill with questions of what life would look like with this new family. What would we eat? Where would I sleep? When and how would I talk to Levi?

I felt disembodied, as if I were watching this day unfold on a movie screen.

I watched with envy as the office staff left to go home to their regular routines. Although they watched this scene of children being removed from their families on a daily basis, I knew there was no way for them to understand the fear and confusion we were feeling.

At last, Connie came to stand in the doorway of the conference room. She was no longer trying to be friendly. Connie was tired too. She simply asked "Ready?" I longed for a cable TV movie moment where she hugs us and tells us "Everything will be fine," however I had worn down Connie's patience. She was as ready for us to leave as we were to go.

We walked out into the parking lot to find a short lady in her forties with bright red spiky hair standing next to an equally bright red SUV. This was Cat, our foster mom.

As we climbed into her SUV, beanie baby cats were everywhere; on the dashboard, suctioned cup to the windows, stuck in cup holders. She laughed as I moved some over to get in the front seat. "Those damn cats slide everywhere, I hate them. But everybody thinks I collect them because of my name." For the first time in hours, I smiled.

I didn't need to worry about filling any awkward silences on the drive to our temporary home. I quickly learned there weren't any silences, awkward or otherwise, with Cat. Her other nickname her husband later informed us was "Chatty Cathy."

Cat told us a little about herself and her family. She was raised Irish Catholic, but no longer went to church. Her and her husband Ron were high school sweethearts and had two biological daughters, Lizzie who was twenty and Morgan who was nine. They had been foster parents for several years and currently had two other placements besides my brother and I, a seventeen-year-old girl named Jennifer and a two-year-old boy named Brayden.

By this time, we had arrived at the bottom of a long winding driveway, leading to the type of house we could only dream of, with a pool and trampoline in the yard, and a huge Rottweiler running towards the car wiggling her butt in happy greeting.

Chapter 28

We entered the house through a formal sitting room. The room was filled with a cream-colored sofa and love seat and a matching cream-colored rug. The walls were filled with wreaths of burgundy flowers and pictures of angels. That room led directly into a formal dining room that had a huge oak table with at least eight chairs each with a fancy place setting. Although the two rooms were decorated beautifully, there was a thin layer of dust on everything.

Cat continued leading us through the house to the family room, "This is where we actually live" she announced. Walking into the open-floor plan family room and kitchen was like walking into a completely different house. Dishes covered the kitchen counters; the small four chair dinette was covered in old school papers and unopened mail. There was laundry piled on the two worn sectionals, a big projection TV blaring cartoons, and a carpet in need of a good vacuum. Nine-year-old Morgan and two-year-old Brayden were dancing and jumping from couch to couch. It was the kind of chaos that only kids from large families would understand. We were quickly introduced and given the grand tour of the house.

My brother being the only boy besides Braydon would have his own room upstairs, I would be staying in a shared space downstairs in the basement. The basement was finished, but still dark and damp. There was no disguising what it was. There were two rooms on one side where the older girls stayed. Jennifer had her own room as she had been with Cat and Ron for almost two years.

I would be sleeping in an open space that was set up with two twin beds and two tall chests for clothes. There weren't any doors in the frames. Just a big open space. On the other side of the stairs was a playroom and a small office and stock room setup. Since Cat was an independent makeup and beauty consultant, the room was filled with her monthly shipments of makeup, skin care and perfume for her to distribute and host in-home parties.

Cat led us further around the corner to where the laundry room was. This was the first time I began to realize that the image set by the formal rooms of the house may be superficial. I tried to hide the way my eyes widened as I turned the corner and stumbled into the knee-high piles of laundry and broken, discarded toys. Cat explained that "It's not usually like this, I just haven't gotten around to sorting things." She explained we would be responsible for our own laundry, including towels and bedding. I asked if there were assigned days and she told me there weren't. We just tried to share and be respectful.

We wrapped up the tour and headed back upstairs. At the top of the stairs, we finally got to meet Ron. He wasn't a big man, but strong and wiry, with a handlebar mustache and curly mullet. He was quiet and calm compared to the talkative and frenetic energy of Cat.

Ron welcomed us to their home. He announced that we would be going to the local diner for dinner. "There is never a day so bad that chicken tenders and a chocolate soda can't fix" he declared. Once we arrived at the restaurant, my brother and I hung back as everyone jostled for seats.

As everyone settled in and placed their orders, I took the opportunity to observe everyone and the way they interacted with each other. Cat and Ron teased each other mercilessly, it was obvious they loved each other. Morgan, their biological daughter, was the center of attention.

She was highly active and talkative like her mom. Braydon had been with Cat and Ron since he was five days old. He was chubby and sweet. He was just starting to say real words and loved to snuggle. Jennifer was intimidating. She had on thick eye make-up and layered chains and chokers. Jennifer had been in and out of foster care most of her life and mastered the tough-guy exterior. I was both terrified and in awe of her. Cat and Ron's other biological daughter, Elizabeth, was twenty and working at the hospital and was going to school for nursing. She was nice but had also seen many kids come through her parents' house, so seemed slightly detached. It was a full house and not like the show on TV.

I did feel myself begin to relax and laugh a little. Ron was right, something about a chocolate soda put the soul at ease.

Chapter 29

It was late in the evening, almost 9 p.m., by the time all of us finished dinner, paid the bill, and loaded back into the vehicle to head home. I could already feel the nervous flutter in my chest. Dinner was a temporary distraction. But now, heading towards bedtime in an unfamiliar place and routine, my worries came tip toeing back. I quietly stared out the window as we drove through the back country roads. It was already dark, so I could mostly see only my face in the reflection. As I stared back at myself, I wondered "How did we get here?" I knew the technical answers. I knew that DCS had every right and good intention in our removal. But my mind wondered deeper than that. My heart wanted to know how and why this had happened. How my parents chose the first step in this long path towards destruction and simply continued walking it. I reflected on the last few months but also wondered what the future would look like. After all, I would be eighteen within a few months. As the fear began to cut my breath short, I scolded myself. My Nanny had told me repeatedly over the last few months that I needed to take each moment as it came. "Second by second, if necessary," she would tell me. I took a deep breath and swallowed past the lump in my throat. I needed to focus on getting through the night.

We arrived back at the house and pulled up the long gravel driveway for the second time that day. Once we made it into the house, everyone dispersed to their regular activities. Cat got busy getting Morgan and Braydon in their pajamas and ready for bed. Ron headed up the hill to the garage to work on a car he was restoring for his father. Elizabeth had made it home from work and was leaning against the kitchen counter eating a salad, still in her scrubs. Jennifer quickly grabbed the cordless phone and headed to our basement room to call her boyfriend.

Bobby and I sat beside each other on the sofa in the family room, staring blankly at the black screen of the turned off television. We were both exhausted by the day, however we were reluctant to be apart. All of our childhood we had a set of orders to follow. Even when we were left home alone there was a set of rules to adhere to and chores to carry out. We didn't know what we were supposed to be doing. So, we sat for a while and watched the chaos of the house unfold around us.

My brother finally gave me a hug and said he was going to go lay down and said I should try to do the same. I sighed and slowly got to my feet. I walked downstairs and sat on the unfamiliar bed with it's strange bedding and gazed at the basement's painted white cement walls. Everything in the room felt cool and damp. There was my twin bed, a small table with a lamp and a dresser with a matching set of furniture at the other end of the room waiting for the next placement. Cat and Ron had a big house and were licensed for up to six placements at one time.

I pulled my pajamas out of my overnight bag and grabbed the towel that Cat had assigned to me. I didn't have any shampoo or body wash; I had only packed the essentials for the planned weekend trip. Thankfully, I had my toothbrush and deodorant, but that was all. I decided I would take a shower regardless. Hot showers have always been a comforting and grounding routine for me.

As I climbed up the stairs to the basement, I had to pass by Cat playing solitaire on her computer. I sat on the step about halfway up, that put me level with her in her desk chair beside the stairs. All night I had waited for some sign of comfort. A hug or an extra word of reassurance. I ached for a mother figure. I sat for a moment until she finally asked me if I needed anything. I quietly asked through tears "Does it ever get easier?" Cat tilted her head and looked at me and said, "I am not sure." I learned in that moment, comfort was not one of Cat's talents. I began to feel embarrassed seeking comfort from a stranger. I was frustrated that I had been in the presence of so many adults and not even one had hugged me or held my hand. Without another word I went upstairs to take my shower. I heard Cat's voice behind me to make sure I kept track of my towel.

I stayed in the shower until the water ran cold. By the time I made my way back downstairs the house was quiet and everyone was asleep in their beds. I was emotionally spent. There were no tears left. I was just tired. I turned on my side and fell asleep.

Chapter 30

My mother was the baby out of four siblings: Nancy, George, and Patricia. My Nanny and Poppy were hard working, strict, but loving parents. Nanny was a stay-at-home mother and Poppy worked third shift at a steel mill until he retired in the early 90's. As a family they worked on a local farm for many years. I grew up hearing many stories of "when we were on the farm." My favorite story is of my two aunts as teenagers. Both had things to do that evening and both were tasked with planting onions. A lot of onions. My aunt Nancy thought that she could get out of it easily by making some of the onions in her bucket disappear. She did so by throwing onion bulbs into the woods by the handful. Nancy got away with it for a while, but before too long the onion sprouts gave up her secrets. There were many such stories of my mom and her siblings growing up. I believe my mom had a happy childhood. Her family didn't have a lot, but she wanted for nothing.

There were many times and many reasons throughout my early childhood that my father didn't have a job. He liked to call himself a "jack of all trades, master of none." That meant that he could do a lot but mostly did nothing. It also meant that there were many holes in our lives to fill. There were many times throughout my childhood where my aunts and grandparents paid for groceries, covered our rent, or paid to keep the lights on when we still lived in Indiana, before moving to Missouri.

When we still attended public school, my Nanny would take my brother and I shopping and buy all our school supplies and clothes for the new school year. My aunt Patricia and her partner Lisa would make a special trip out for our birthdays each year. They would pick us up and take us out to eat at the restaurant of our choice and let us pick out a new pair of shoes.

Growing up, my extended family was the reason my brother and I believed in the magic of Christmas. Even as kids, we knew that our parents barely had the money to provide for our basic needs, let alone extravagant luxuries like new baby dolls or an R/C car. Waking up Christmas morning and tip toeing down the hall to see all our presents was truly wondrous. We knew instantly what Santa had brought us because all the presents were unwrapped and unboxed. My mom always told us that was so we could just wake up and start playing with our new toys, Santa knew we wouldn't want to waste time. I found out from my aunt Lisa, that the reality was the family unboxed every new toy they bought us, otherwise my parents would return them to the store to receive the cash before we would ever see them.

My mom knew that no matter how low she fell, her family would always be there to catch her and pick up the slack. This time wouldn't be any different.

While my brother and I were settling in and learning to navigate our way through our new foster family, my aunts and grandparents were busy trying their best to set my mom up for success according to the protection plan put in place by Family Services. Some of the things on that check list were easy enough to remedy. My mom already had a job and transportation, but she needed an apartment. One of her own, without Stan.

After Connie the caseworker had laid out clearly what needed to be done, my aunt Nancy left on a mission. My aunt Nancy is notorious in our family for her bossy nature. When Nancy lays out the plans, they are followed. Nancy returned to Indiana and called an immediate family meeting. Nancy and Bruce, Nanny and Poppy, along with Patricia and Lisa met at the shared lake house. Nancy informed Patricia and Lisa of all that had happened.

The very first thing that Patricia and Lisa did was contact an attorney. They wanted us. Patricia and Lisa were willing to do whatever it took to gain custody of my brother and me and they were not going to take no for an answer. However, by the time the attorney was contacted and proceedings were put in motion, my brother and I were already wards of the state. That meant that that the state of Ohio held guardianship of us although our parents kept legal custody.

That information put them back at square one because, although they wanted us home with them as quick as possible, there was also the risk of complicating something that should be over rather quickly. If the terms of the plan were met.

My three aunts made a plan. They would return to Ohio the next weekend to put my mom on the right track.

My family found her an apartment and cosigned for the lease. Each of my aunts and my grandparents decided they would split my mom's bills. They divided her household bills between the four of them and ended up paying for her for the next eight months until my dad went to prison.

The second week we were in foster care, my mother, with the help of her family, moved from the house she shared with my father. For the first time in over twenty years my parents were physically and legally separated.

No one knows where my dad hid out that weekend. But he very wisely stayed away. Although my mom claimed to her family that she had already separated from him, there were hints to his presence throughout the home as they were packing. His clothes in the hamper, his toothbrush in the bathroom, two dishes in the sink.

My mom promised them that she would stick to the plan. She promised them that nothing would stand between her getting my brother and I back where we belonged, which was with her.

My family demanded of DCS that they be able to visit with Bobby and I before returning to Indiana. DCS compromised and gave us a two-hour supervised visit at the DCS office. After a long ten days, we all were reunited.

Chapter 31

One of life's greatest mysteries was the love my parent's shared with each other. Their love felt like a fifth person in our family. It was a separate entity. I didn't feel like a product of that love, instead I felt like more of an intrusion.

Stan and Beverly were high school sweethearts. Stan was a charming boy who was raised by a poor, divorced, single mom from the wrong side of town. Beverly was smart and a member of the business clubs at the high school. Their relationship was a terribly kept secret for three years. Beverly would sneak downstairs at night to talk to Stan on the phone late into the night. They would meet up secretly at the local roller-skating rink. Most of their communication was handwritten letters and poems. I longed for the day my mom would share those letters with me. I felt sure that if I could read their special words to each other, I would begin to understand the wonder of their relationship. My mom would never share those letters with me. Every time we moved and the box was unearthed, she would quickly tape up the box and push it aside. At first, I thought it was because they were special and private. Even then I found her secretive behavior so odd. Didn't most mothers long for the day they could share their love story with their children? I would later learn that those words were less magical and more manipulative and sexual.

Stan graduated the year before Beverly in 1983 and promptly enlisted in the Army. He did come from a long line of veterans, but also it seemed like a quick route to a life of acceptance and respect.

The year that Stan was in basic training was a difficult one for Beverly. Another year filled with those love letters and clandestine plans for their future. There was never any doubt in the young couples' minds that they would marry one another and be together forever.

Beverly graduated in May of 1984. Stan came home on leave a few weeks later and they were married by the third week in June. Their wedding ceremony was simple and held at the local park in the small town in Indiana where they grew up. Friends and family surrounded them, although not all were attending happily. The wedding pictures were kept in an old sapphire blue photo album. I clearly remember the frowns of unhappiness on the faces of my grandparents. I would spend hours looking through those pictures, searching for clues as to who these two people were, what they were feeling, and how they differed from the people who were my parents.

Not long after the wedding, Beverly boarded a plane to Germany to join Stan at his duty station. Both of my parents spoke fondly of their time in Germany. Finally, they were able to be together without rules or parental oversight. I didn't hear a lot of stories about Germany. But there were a few things my mom would tell me. She would tell me how the landlord required her to sweep the sidewalk daily in the morning and evening in front of their apartment, that beer was served everywhere in Germany, that it was a beautiful country and that she always wanted to return.

Following the age-old rhyme: First comes love, second comes marriage, then in the fall of 1985 came Alice in a baby carriage.

My mom spent most of her pregnancy in Germany. At the very last moment, she flew home. She arrived back in Indiana in the fall of 1985 without my dad. I was set to be born sometime in the beginning of November.

Every child has a birth story that the family shares. The lore and magic of the day they were born. My birth story starts on a sunny fall morning. My mom went out to rake leaves and help with yard work. After several hours of work and a big dinner, she made her way upstairs for a restless night of sleep.

The next morning, mom made her way down the narrow staircase of her childhood home for breakfast. As she rounded the corner, my nanny gasped "What happened?" At some point during the night, I had done a flip in my mother's womb. I went from head down birthing position to footling breach. My mother's belly had gone from a round basketball shape to an oval egg like shape. And thus, labor began.

I grew up hearing the horror stories of the C-section my mom endured to bring me into this world. Most of the stories I heard of my infancy and toddlerhood were more of how my actions or even existence affected my mom rather than tales of my precocious cuteness.

On some levels, my parents' lives changed with my birth, but in many ways, they remained "Stan and Beverly." Although now they towed a car seat and diaper bag along with them.

My parents' relationship felt awkward to outsiders. There was always a feeling of indecency. Even after our family became active in church, their inside jokes between themselves and occasionally with other couples, always pushed the boundaries. There was always an undercurrent of manipulation, both of each other and those around them. Being in the presence of their relationship felt risky, it didn't feel comfortable.

I felt like I grew up in the shadow of their relationship. There was never a question that they came first and everyone and everything else landed wherever they fell. Many times, especially when I was a teenager, my mom would express how the husband should always come first.

My parent's relationship was also very volatile. I never saw physical abuse between them, however, there were often loud arguments between them.

Early in their marriage, my mother knew that if she left him, her family would step up and fill the gaps to help her get back on her feet. And she would readily use that fact against him. Later, after secrets began to fill the nooks and crannies of their marriage, I believe my father would use the fact of her family's disappointment against her.

Most days were filled with bickering. I learned to walk on eggshells to avoid any confrontations. It felt like every car ride was accompanied with heavy and tense silences. But when we arrived at the destination, we all hopped out with smiles plastered on our faces. No matter what, the world must never know what goes on behind closed doors.

My parents' love for one another was a river; deep, mysterious, raging, and unpredictable. It provided life for them but the rest of us were swept away by it.

Chapter 32

My mother was the center of my world. My days began and ended with her. As a young child, I hated for her to be out of my sight. Early in my childhood, my mom worked as a switchboard operator at the local hospital. Every time she left for her shift, I would feel untethered and lost. Whenever my mom left me, she would always leave something of hers with me, like her jacket or a piece of her jewelry. I was convinced that she would always come back for the thing she left with me, but I never believed she would come back for me. I never really grew out of that. I simply learned how to hide the panic I felt.

As I grew, I continued to search for that comfort and unconditional love from my mom. Her love for me felt finicky. It was well known that my brother Bobby was her baby. My brother and I were born in the late eighties. There were no gender reveal parties until after the baby was born. My mom made no secret of the fact that she wanted a boy when she was carrying me. She also made a big deal over Bobby being her "last baby."

My mom didn't hate me, but I do believe that she was jealous of me. All her life she had been the baby of the family. Everyone doted on her, even her siblings and especially her dad. It was no question to anyone that Poppy was his happiest when he was surrounded by his grandchildren. It was also no secret that there was a special twinkle in his eye reserved only for me.

My mom was an expert at being passive aggressive. As far back as I can remember, my mom has told me she hates Christmas. She hated decorating, shopping, and especially the music. For the longest time I thought it was because we were living in Missouri and were far from our family. Or it was because there was never enough money, so it was stressful trying to buy gifts. Although, usually my aunts and grandparents took care of that or once we moved to Missouri, churches we attended filled those gaps. One day I just asked her, "Mom, why do you hate Christmas?" And this is the story she told me:

The year I turned three, I asked for a PlaySkool kitchen for Christmas. It was the only thing I asked Santa for. Christmas morning came and I ran to the tree to find a red and white wooden kitchen set, complete with a few plastic and tin dishes. According to the story, my three-year-old self declared that I hated it and marched out of the room.

I remember none of this. I do remember playing with the kitchen set, which I realize now was probably a hand-me down from my cousin, because it matched my baby doll's crib and highchair. My memories were of happily playing "house" for hours. But for the rest of my life, my mom let that moment of toddler frustration and emotion spoil our Christmas memories.

Around the time I turned twelve, the dynamic between us began to change. I have never been certain whether my mom was aware of what went on behind closed doors at night in her home. My mom swears she never knew. In my heart, I believe she knew, despite her numerous denials over the years.

I desperately wanted to believe that my mother didn't know. I couldn't imagine a reality where a mother *knew* her child was being violated and knowingly turn away from it. As I became an adult and experienced sharing a marriage bed with a partner, I realized that it's exceedingly difficult to ignore the absence of your partner in bed. Maybe you won't be disturbed by a quick trip to the bathroom, but when their side of the bed is empty for hours on a nightly basis over the course of many years, you would notice. As I became a mother, I realized how attuned you become to your child's moods and behaviors, yet my mother never noticed my fear, reluctance, and repulsion when it came to my interactions with my dad. I will never know with certainty because my mother will never tell. But this is my belief.

As I entered my teen years, my mom and I would walk a strange path. At times she would keep me close. We would go to the library together and discuss books. Our shopping trips would begin with getting vanilla cokes from the food court and then browsing through all the shops in the mall. One of our favorite traditions was sharing a pumpkin pie ice cream every fall.

But, just as she would pull me close, there were some days where she kept me at arm's length. Days where it felt that my presence alone was offensive to her.

When we moved from Missouri to Ohio, to be a part of Paul and Emily's church, her friendship with Emily deepened.

Our family met Paul and Emily in Missouri when we attended the same church. Paul and Emily were recently licensed for foster care and needed a full-time childcare provider for their foster daughters. Since homeschooling made my schedule flexible, I was a perfect fit. Our families began spending more time together. Emily and I became remarkably close, but the young couple also grew close to my parents.

About a year after we met, Paul and Emily accepted a position back in the small town in Ohio, where Emily grew up. By this time, it had been decided that my parents were going to quit school. They didn't have enough credit hours to graduate and had maxed out their student loans. Over the five years they had been attending college, my parents would reapply and accept the maximum amount of loan money offered to them each semester. They would use these funds to catch up their delinquent bills and splurge on unnecessary purchases. We had no reason to stay in Missouri, but nowhere else to really go. Paul approached his congregation in Ohio, and they offered my parents the position of youth pastor and choir director.

So, once again, we packed everything in a truck and moved across the country. We moved into a tiny house down the road from the church . In fact, the house we moved into was once a chicken coop!

Emily's oldest daughter attended a Christian school that was 45 minutes away. Three mornings a week, Emily would drop off her two younger girls and pick up my mom. I would oversee Emily's kids and my brother while her and my mom would have "prayer meetings." It would be afternoon before they returned.

Those days weren't so bad because my dad would be at work. It was the nights when Emily would pick my mom up to run to the grocery store and I would be left with my dad that I hated.

The closest retail chain grocery store was 20 minutes away in a nearby town only slightly bigger than ours. Emily would call my mom after her kids were in bed and ask her to ride with her. As soon as I would hear the phone ring in the evening, I would feel my dinner rise in the back of my throat. I was 15 years old, but I would begin to whine as if I were five. I would beg to be allowed to go with them, I would even stay in the van. It wasn't that I wanted so bad to go or to shop, or even be included in their adult conversations, I just didn't want to be left alone with my dad. My mom, on a rare occasion, allowed me to go. I would mostly spend those evenings quietly in my bedroom, afraid to even go out to the bathroom, hoping that out of sight was out of mind.

The revelation of my secret led to an interesting turn of events in my mother's life. A circumstance which had been repetitive for her. Our relationship turned a corner that it would never be able to return from. My mom felt that *I* took everything from her. I became the *other woman*, both in her marriage and her relationship with her best friend. I once again became the reason for a fracture in her relationship with her family.

Chapter 33

Our first week at Cat and Ron's felt like being dropped into an alternate universe. During the day, the house was quiet because the older kids were in school, Ron was at work, and Lizzie was sleeping for her night shift at the hospital. Cat would be watching TV in the living room while Brayden ran around as any active two-year-old does.

I tip-toed upstairs on that first morning and blinked in the sunshine streaming in the patio doors that led in from the back deck to the open floor plan family room and kitchen. I quietly sat on the sofa and watched the activity in the room. I was hungry but didn't know how to ask about breakfast. It is a strange and uncomfortable feeling when somewhere is supposed to feel like home, yet nothing is familiar. I didn't expect to wake up to Carol Brady making pancakes and bacon; however, I did expect a certain level of hospitality from someone who had been fostering for as long as Cat had. I was seventeen years old; I didn't expect to be waited on. But despite the fact I was in foster care and came from an abusive situation, my brother and I were very well mannered. I didn't even open the refrigerator at *my home* without asking permission. A tour of the kitchen and pantry would have eased my anxiety. Cat could have simply said "Here are bowls, milk is in the fridge, cereals in the cupboard," and that would have given me the permission and ability to care for myself and Bobby.

But it wasn't that simple. The small four-chair dinette that sat between the kitchen and the family room was piled high with mail and various detritus from everyone walking in the door from school and work and dropping whatever they had carried in. The kitchen counters were covered in several days of dirty dishes, where the kids had fed themselves but not cleaned up after themselves.

It was almost 45 minutes before Cat noticed I was sitting there, "Oh. Hey. I didn't even know you were here. You can see if there is any food in there you like, but I haven't been to the store so there probably isn't much." I would quickly come to realize that there never was very much. Cat hardly ever went to the grocery store, there were rarely dinners made for the whole family, and for Cat to even be downstairs and out of her bedroom was a strange event.

I knew that I would need to just step in and take care of whatever task I needed, or one of the little ones needed. Within a few days of my being there, Cat saw that Brayden and I easily bonded, so I became the one to care for him. The first morning I didn't know where to get my own breakfast, by the third morning I was going to Cat's third floor master bedroom suite to get the baby, taking him downstairs with me, fixing breakfast for the two of us and cleaning up the mess from the night before.

Within the first few days not only did Connie come by to meet with us and update us on our case, but we also met our second case worker. Connie worked for DFS, but Rachel worked for a separate foster care agency that Cat and Ron were licensed through. Rachel was the opposite of Connie. Rachel was in her late twenties and very pretty. She was tall and had brown hair she pulled back with a barrette. Rachel reminded me of Miss Honey from the movie Matilda, both in physical appearance and in mannerisms. Connie would be visiting us monthly at Cat's house, but Rachel would visit us weekly. On these visits, Rachel would take us out to lunch, shopping, to a movie, or to a park. Any kind of activity that would be fun for us. Connie's goals were to make sure we behaved and were receiving the services we needed. Rachel's goals were to make sure we were doing okay, that we felt safe, and our needs were being met.

Rachel was one of my biggest advocates. She went above and beyond to make sure I had what I needed. She knew that not having clothes and toiletries was weighing very heavily on me. When a child receives a state stipend, it can take up to three weeks to arrive. Rachel was able to get mine expedited, so I received it by the end of my second week in foster care. For the clothing part of the stipend, we received a $300 voucher to our choice between department stores. Cat said I should choose the most high-end store. I didn't really care where the clothes came from as long as I had them, so I did as she suggested. The toiletries part was sent in a check form to the foster parent. By the end of the second week, I had soap and clothes. I wouldn't say that I was happy, but I did feel better being clean.

The best thing that happened by the end of the second week is we got to finally see our family. We were only allowed supervised visits at the DCS office at this time. So, we all piled into a small room with a one-way mirrored window.

The room had a few battered chairs and they had pulled in a few office chairs to accommodate our family. My mom was there and all three of my aunts, my uncle, and my grandparents. It was obvious that the room was set up for younger kids. There were baskets of toys and kid's books in the corner and one of those giant wooden activity cubes with the beads on top like you would see in a doctor's office.

The first tearful face I saw was my aunt Nancy's. I walked straight into her arms and collapsed to her lap. I could feel her arms tight around me and hear the sniffles from the others in the room. I eventually made my way around the room, hugging my uncle Bruce, my aunts' Patricia and Lisa, my Nanny and Poppy, and finally my mom.

The tension was heavy. It had been a terribly long week for all of us. My family had spent the week moving my mom from her apartment that she shared with my dad, to one of her own. The anger was also plain. It was obvious that my mom's sisters had spent a good portion of the week lecturing her and questioning her on all that had transpired. Their main question being "How could she let this happen?" My mom stood firm in her denial of knowledge. They extracted promises of her to remain separated from our father. "Please just stay away from him" was their constant refrain.

We didn't speak much during the two-hour visit. Partly because it felt weird to discuss anything knowing we were being watched and listened to, but also, we just didn't know what to say. Poppy broke the ice by asking about where we were staying and asking if we had what we needed. We told him we did and showed him our new clothes and shoes.

I had avoided eye contact with my mom. As much as I missed her and had longed to see and talk to her over the last ten days, I also was starting to feel anger and confusion. I began to question what was going to happen, what were the details, what was the plan?

My aunt Nancy took control of the conversation and began to explain that we had to stay. We would not be able to come home, but it shouldn't take long. That was what everyone kept saying. That's all they said. My family, my mom, caseworkers, Cat. "You won't be here long." "Don't worry, you will be going home soon." "Your case is not too complicated; it won't take long."

The visit began to fade into tense silence, broken by sniffles and pats to my back. My Nanny complimented my new jeans. This was my first-time wearing jeans in front of my mom since I was nine years old. It was my small rebellion. My family had seen me in jeans, as I had started wearing them while staying with my aunt, but I had still worn skirts the few times I would see my mom. By wearing the jeans on our first visit was my way of beginning the separation in my heart.

One of my biggest concerns since we had been removed was that I had not been able to speak to Levi. This was the first time in our relationship that we had been without contact. I knew Levi would be distraught because I just hadn't called. We weren't allowed to talk to anyone until Connie and my parents had discussed all the permissions of what my parents would allow and not allow while we were in foster care.

You see, even though my parents were deemed unfit to have us in their custody, they still had parental rights and made all decisions on our care. Even with the charges my dad was facing, he was still included in all decisions and updates on our well-being. In the beginning, my dad even stipulated that we attend church. We also had to seek permission to get a haircut, visit a friend, anything that would require parental permission in a home setting was still decided by our parents, not our foster parents.

All I knew is the day before we left Indiana to return to Ohio, I had my normal nightly call to Levi. And then nothing. Finally on the day of our supervised visit I was able to find out what was going on. Levi had stopped at nothing to find out what was going on. He had called both my mom and Nancy until they finally answered and filled him in on what had happened. I would finally be able to speak to him that evening.

We wrapped up the visit with details of our next visit, scheduled phone calls, and hugs all around.

My aunts and grandparents were returning to Indiana. They were leaving my mom on her own. They promised she would do the right thing.

We returned to Cat's house. It hit me like a ton of bricks, that this was my new normal. There wasn't a switch that could be flipped. No ruby red slippers to click together. I wasn't going home any time soon.

Chapter 34

There are many challenges in the life of a child in an abusive or neglectful home. Several of those challenges begin when the child is removed from the home situation and placed in foster care. Foster care is an extreme balancing act for a child.

Every family has its own dynamics. These dynamics are built by the values, events, and conversations that make up our daily lives. Many of you have probably heard the parable of the young wife and her pot roast. If not, I will indulge you: A young woman is preparing an expensive cut of beef. Her husband walks in and sees she is cutting off the ends of the roast. The husband is astonished. "Honey, that costs a lot of our hard-earned money, what are you doing?" She goes on to tell him she is preparing her mother's famous pot roast. "But why have you cut off the ends?" She pauses and says "Well, that's how my mother always does it." So, they call up her mother to ask for the reason and she replies, "That's how my mother has always done it." They then call and repeat the question to Grandma and she says, "I am not sure why the two of you cut the ends off of yours, I cut off mine because I didn't have a big enough roasting pan."

That story always brings a smile to my face. But also, it sets an incredibly good example of how dynamics run through the generations of a family. Even when those dynamics are unhealthy, uncomfortable, and dangerous we tend to cling to them because they belong to us. It is well known that we, as people, fear the unknown, so many times we hold on to what is toxic because it is less scary than what we don't know.

Entering an unfamiliar family dynamic feels like entering a foreign country. The house smells different, the routines run on odd time frames, the food is strange. Even the language can feel unusual with its own slang, idioms, and inside jokes. Navigating these new dynamics on their own is a difficult, yet attainable task. However, when you factor in not only the age, the abrupt removal, or, perhaps most importantly, the reasons for the removal of that child from their family and their homes, that task of adjustment becomes exponentially more complicated.

Many times, as adults we forget to look at the situations that the little ones in our lives deal with from their vantage point. The circumstances that bring these children into the foster care system are undeniably difficult. These children have been carrying a weight too heavy for them and hiding secrets we could never fathom. Yet, upon entering a new home so many times we expect a level of behavior and understanding that not even we, as adults, can manifest.

Children entering the system often are expected to be relieved, to be well behaved and most importantly to be grateful. I believe that mostly these children *are* grateful and relieved. But also, they are confused, wary, and tired.

The first and most important thing to consider is the loyalty that a child feels towards their birth parents. Humans are inherently loyal to our parents from birth. It is a form of self-preservation. Dr. Regina Sullivan, a Developmental Behavior Neuroscientist, discusses how newborns spend the first hours of their lives acclimating to their surroundings. Observing wide-eyed and quiet, the sights, sounds, and smells that make up their environment. But more importantly, the sights, sounds, and smells that identify their caretakers. And so, the bond begins.

Logically we may ask ourselves whether self-preservation would cause that child to refrain from bonding with a caretaker that may bring harm to them. For a very long time, researchers and scientist assumed that this phenomenal attachment is due to the immaturity of the infant and their developing brain. However, recently it has been determined that the infant's brain is perfectly capable, even as a newborn, to carry out the tasks appropriate to their survival needs. Meaning the newborn can't feed itself, however it can cry to notify its caregiver of its need for food. An infant and young child is not physically capable of meeting its own needs; however, its brain can make the necessary connections to meet its needs for survival.

What this essentially means is that the danger switch effectively turns off when it comes to the caretaker, simply because they are the means to the child's survival. This is an essential issue when it comes to children of any age entering foster care.

I was seventeen years old when I went into care. I had been out of the abusive situation for almost a year. I was very aware that the abuse and neglect that I suffered at the hand of my parents was criminal and toxic. However, I still felt a fidelity to them that encompassed every aspect of my young life. My biggest fear was that by allowing the small glimpses of love and kindness from my foster parents, I was betraying them. As I began to receive my court-ordered psychiatric care, I felt immense amounts of guilt for even discussing my childhood with my therapist. To the point that it hindered any help I might have received from that care.

I also witnessed this with one of my foster sisters. Nevaeh was two years old when she was placed with us at Cat and Ron's. We all fell in love with her adorable, spunky, chubby-cheeked personality instantly. Nevaeh had the hardest time bonding with Cat. She would repeatedly tell her "You not mommy." Nevaeh had suffered severe neglect from her birth mother. She had an older biological sister who suffered from fetal alcohol syndrome. Both girls clung to the idea of their birth mother.

Eventually the mother went to prison on unrelated charges, at that point, the girls did begin to ease into the formed relationships once the short-term memory of toddlerhood set in.

I believe that not only understanding these feelings of loyalty and betrayal, but also accepting them, are important to the success of the acclimation into the new home for these children. I think it's imperative for caregivers of these children to help them understand how natural this response is. Understanding how our brains and bodies respond to trauma and neglect can be a crucial step in alleviating some of the guilt and shame these children already carry in their daily lives.

I believe that it is ingrained in our very souls to connect with our origins. To know our stories and what makes us who we are. I believe that children, especially in foster care and adoptive situations, will experience that need on an exceptional level. It is crucial to their identity to know and understand where and from whom they come. It is also important for us, as adults, to help them understand that the sins of their mothers and fathers, are not to be carried on the shoulders of their children. There is no action or decision that a parent makes that their children should hold accountability for, because they are just children.

Which brings me to the next challenge, the behavior of a child in foster care. Every child's situation is unique. Some children come from homes with militant control of everything they do, say, wear, and even eat. With extreme physical and emotional punishment for any errant behavior. Others may come from a home of complete and utter chaos. These homes often are places where cleanliness and behavior are at the whim of the adults in the home. Consider these examples as opposite sides of a spectrum with many instances in between.

The behavior of a child should never decide the level of care and compassion a child receives. Children of trauma use behavior as a means of communication in situations where they don't have the means and maturity to process their environment.

As adults, we sometimes forget how overwhelming it is just to be small. Not to mention the added burden of trauma. These children have no control and a lot of times no voice. Children learn very quickly how to make themselves heard.

In my experience, often there is the idea that children entering foster care should be thankful and on their best behavior. I believe it is important for the adults providing care to these children see it as a service of compassion instead of badge of honor and heroism.

There are many wonderful foster care providers. There are many who understand that these children have received so little in love and assurance. You may have to continue to offer your love over and over. You will be disrespected, disobeyed, and disliked. Children will often push their boundaries. They want to know what it will take for you to lash out, hurt them, and give up on them. They are only able to act out the worn-out paths of toxicity and abuse over and over. Until someone in their lives cares enough to be patient, understanding, and strong. Someone who will stand beside them and walk with them as they learn how to break the cycles of their past generations.

Chapter 35

The ride home from our first supervised visit was quiet. There weren't many opportunities of quiet living at Cat and Ron's. Sitting in the quiet, I began to recognize the reality of my situation. The constant scrambling in my brain to find a solution or way out began to subside. I knew I was just going to have to make the best of it. There was nothing I could control; I no longer had a say in what happened to or around me. I learned to adapt.

Spring quickly turned into long summer days and I settled into a routine. There were a lot of projects that sat unfinished around the house: a playroom and kitchen that needed organized, the laundry room needed cleaned, and the formal dining room needed to be deep cleaned. There was an extensive list of things that needed done that Cat couldn't or didn't want to be bothered with.

Cat was not a terrible person. She was not an awful mother to her kids, biological or fostered. Cat had her own mental health issues to fight against. First being adult ADHD. Cat couldn't stay on task; she would start a huge project such as the laundry room. The laundry room was a large room in the basement. It held a brand-new top of the line washer and dryer, cute wicker laundry baskets, extra-large bottles of name brand laundry soap and fabric softener, shelves for folding, racks for hanging, and giant piles of clothes. Clean clothes, dirty clothes, clothes from past placements, clothes that Morgan had outgrown, just piles and piles of clothes. What happened? Well, about two years previously,

Cat had decided to remodel the laundry room. If it looked nice and pretty, she believed she would be more likely to do laundry. Except that halfway through she got bored, and then Braydon was placed with her as an infant, then Cat's mother passed away and she became severely depressed.

That was Cat's other major mental health issue: depression. When Cat was depressed, she didn't leave her room. Period. She simply didn't get out of bed. One of us would take her drinks, cigarettes, and snacks. By one of us, I mean me. It was pretty much always me. There was a TV so she could watch her psychics on daytime talk shows. That was just normal to everyone that lived in the household. She would come hustling down the stairs spraying on perfume fifteen minutes after we should have left to be wherever we were supposed to go. And we all just existed around her like tiny little moons.

So, Cat and I made a deal. She would pay me $100 every month when she got her stipend check for fostering if I would help finish all the projects around the house. I agreed. I needed the money.

The collective of adults in charge of my life agreed that if Levi and I could figure out how to get to one another we could spend one full day, until 10 p.m. together, every other weekend. They didn't think we would be determined enough to do it. Levi and I were 45 minutes apart. Neither one of us had a job or driver's license, so we had to earn the money and then pay his aunt to drive halfway to pick me up and drop me off.

The relationship between Cat and I would remain strained during my time in her home. There were many times when our relationship flourished. But there were many other times when I looked to her to fill the role of a mother, and she simply couldn't. I was desperate for a mother's touch and support. I searched for it in so many areas in my life and it just wasn't anywhere to be found.

Foster care was hard. I know that seems like a silly thing to say. But sometimes the simplest expression is the truest. There were so many concerns to juggle. There were appointments, relationships, trauma, and every day survival tasks.

The days stacked up on top of each other. Rachel, our agency case worker, visited my brother and I weekly. She would take us to breakfast or to the library. Rachel would always ask us what we would like to do or where we would like to go. My brother and I never knew what to suggest. Rachel would tell us we could go to the movies, bowling, or skating. We didn't realize that the agency paid for these activities. We thought she had been paying for them out of her pocket, so my brother and I felt terribly awkward asking to do any activities. We did love seeing Rachel every week though. She was a breath of fresh air. Rachel was one of the few people in my life at this time that I felt I could be honest with, was honest with me, and supported me unconditionally.

We also had supervised visits twice a week. Both my mom and Cat complained about the inconvenience of these visits. My mom complained about having to arrange her work schedule around the visits. She also was very offended at the idea of needing supervised visits at all. Cat complained because of the time and distance to get to the DCS office twice a week.

For me, this caused a lot of guilt and dread. I longed for visits with my mom. I missed her incredibly. But because both her and Cat were so vocal about how terrible the visits were for them, I just dreaded it. I felt guilty for causing that much frustration for them both.

After about 30 days in foster care, my mom and Cat found one thing to see eye-to-eye on: ending the visits at DCS. Somehow, together, they convinced Connie, who convinced the judge, to allow Cat to now be the supervisor of our visits. That meant that mom could visit us anywhere that was convenient for everyone, if Cat were present. My mom was allowed to come to Cat's house, or we could meet at a restaurant, the library, anywhere that we felt we could spend quality time together. A common meeting place, due to convenience, was the gym where Morgan had gymnastics practice.

Following the trend, visits with my mom declined significantly when there wasn't an authority holding her accountable. When Cat and Connie told me that my mom would now be able to visit us at our placement and any time, for any length of time, I was excited. To my knowledge, my dad was finally out of all our lives and I felt like my mom, brother and I would finally get the opportunity to start to heal, bond, and create a new family dynamic.

This was how the summer was spent. During the week I attended my appointments, case worker meetings, cleaning the house, and counting the minutes to visits with my mom and Saturdays with Levi. This was what was happening on the surface, but there was so much more going on underneath.

Chapter 36

I began receiving my court-ordered therapy about six weeks into my placement in foster care. This was a struggle for me on several levels. I was incredibly skeptical. The only experience of counseling I had up to this point were two, very underwhelming and unsuccessful attempts by different church leaders. This led to another reason for skepticism. In my experience of the Baptist church, we were taught that a diminished mental health was a weakness in our relationship with the Lord. Mental health was just another area in my life where I carried guilt of not being good enough or strong enough to conquer.

My mental health was spiraling. Although most every adult in my life knew what was going on and why I was where I was, they continued to express surprise at the idea that I was not feeling well. I tried with all my might to put on a brave face. But entering foster care knocked a great deal of the wind from my sails. Not sleeping led to hours of sitting alone in the dark of my basement bedroom. This was the first time that I felt suicidal. I had a history of cutting and self-harm. However, that behavior never had an intention beyond feeling in control and a feeling of release. By inflicting the pain on myself, it released some of the pressure I felt in my soul. But never during those times did I consider what the world would be like if I were no longer a part of it.

But now I did. I imagined the relief of simply no longer being. The relief that everyone would feel if the problem, which I considered to be myself, was just gone.

I struggled with eating. Mostly I just didn't eat or ate very little. Not eating had nothing to do with weight or body image and everything to do with control. I couldn't control any of the outside circumstances in my life, but I could control what I put into my body and when. The feeling of hunger worked much in the same way as the pain from self-harming. It supplied a kind of release valve, as well as something for me to focus on besides the ever-present racing heart and breathlessness of constant anxiety. The side effects of hunger such as headaches, trembling, dizziness, and the cuts and scratches from self-harming also made a visible and physical presentation of the pain I felt inside. They were outward signs that I hoped people around me could see if they took the time to observe. Sadly, these cries for help went mostly unheard.

I began writing in a secret journal. It was a secret because no one could know how I felt. I was ashamed that I couldn't control these thoughts and feelings. That I couldn't pray away the sadness and darkness. There were also two other reasons for secrecy. The first reason being my case had not yet been to court, so everything was considered evidence. The second reason, I knew if anyone knew about these feelings they would be horrified. I was terrified that if found out, the authorities in my life such as Rachel and Connie, would medicate me, or worse, hospitalize me. Medication would have probably given me help and relief. However, my parents had made it clear that medicating anything that was not a physical ailment was wrong and sinful.

The entries in this journal were a truly clear timeline of the descent of my emotional and mental well-being. There were pages filled with my cries for help, of desperation and loneliness. I also expressed myself through song lyrics. One page was filled with only curse words. Over and over again. Many pages were filled with spirals. That is the only feeling I could identify with. I felt scared and out of control.

I wanted to share all these feelings with my counselor. But I couldn't. The words would not leave my mouth.

My counselor asked me to call her Rhonda on our very first visit. She was warm, kind and very pregnant. Her office was small and decorated tastefully in quiet colors and paintings of water. The first few sessions we simply talked of everyday things. One of the main topics we discussed is how much I struggled with my foster sisters. Especially Jennifer. Jenn had been with Cat and Ron for a long time, she wasn't used to sharing the spotlight. I didn't mean to take the attention away from her. However, by nature I was a child who thrived on the positive reinforcement that came from good behavior. Jennifer used to tease me about being a goody two shoes. These were things I felt comfortable discussing. I slowly began to trust Rhonda. I would find myself slipping in dark details between our regular conversations. I was like a scared animal. If she looked at my issue directly, I would scurry back to my corner and hide.

I was constantly on guard of the words I said. I was very aware of the fact that she was reporting. Remember: everything was evidence. I could never be unguarded. My parents had convinced me that no one was there to help me. Everyone in my life was working to gain evidence against my dad.

Rhonda did her best to ask me questions, to try to lead me to a place where we could begin to unravel all the knots that had become my life. No matter what she did, I couldn't allow myself to trust her. I didn't know where to begin or how to express everything that I had been made to keep a secret for most of my life.

I was angry and ashamed. I didn't feel like I deserved the help being offered to me. Rhonda was nice. However, she didn't push. If she asked a question and I refused to answer or changed the subject, she would back down.

A common phrase in the notes of all my service providers was that "Alice seems to be extremely well adjusted considering her history." This would be a theme that would continue to follow me to adulthood. I had learned incredibly early in life to hide my emotions and mask any negative effects that I felt. Unfortunately, because I didn't rage or cry hysterically and instead, smiled, and complied with anything I was asked, I didn't receive the help that I needed to heal and actually become as well adjusted as they thought I was.

My brain and body were trying to cope with years of confusion and warring emotions. My body was rushed into adulthood by the abuse from my father, however, my emotional maturity was stuck in neutral. I would struggle for many years to process emotions at proper maturity, especially strong emotions such as grief, fear, and anger.

Not only was I trying to heal from the years of abuse and secrecy. But I was also trying to process my everyday life, which at this point had been far from normal for over a year. Even my life in foster care had been an exhausting foray, trying to navigate all the emotions that come from living in a home with several traumatized teenagers, led by a mother figure dealing with her own mental health issues.

Several times my mother was invited and encouraged to attend sessions with Rhonda and me. As I had come to expect, she never got around to joining us. There were always excuses. Her main one being that it was hard to get time off work for all the obligations she now had due to us being in the state's custody.

I felt so alone and abandoned. There was never a single adult that looked beyond the surface. No one that said, "this child is in pain, she is struggling, how can we help her?" There was no one that reached out a hand to hold or a hug and simply say "you're going to be okay."

I felt hopeless and desolate. I didn't know how I was going to find the strength to make it through. I continued to take one step, one second, at a time. I hoped that each step forward would eventually lead me to a path out of the darkness.

Chapter 37

The day of Stan's trial was hot and humid. One of those days where it is hard to catch your breath. It could have been snowing that day and I would have still struggled to catch my breath. The evening before, my foster mom helped lay out my clothes for the next day's events. I was seventeen and wanted to look as much like an adult as I could. I chose pale pink slacks and a soft sleeveless cream sweater. My hair was long and curly. My aunt Nancy had paid to have a spiral perm put in while I was staying with her before foster care.

As I said, I wanted to look grown up, so my foster mom, Cat, and I straightened my long thick hair. It took hours and I was afraid that the humidity would make it curl up again.

I don't remember much about the 40-minute drive. My brother, my foster mom, her adult biological daughter, and I were attending the trial. We had only been in care about two months, so while I appreciated their support, they still felt like strangers.

The four of us were ushered into a small office about a block diagonal from the huge courthouse.

We sat in a waiting room. As an adult, I sometimes wonder what the women in the office thought of me that day. What did they say to us? I don't recall. I remember Cat having a whispered conversation with our case worker who had met us there. I remember flipping through my Bible reading different verses in Psalms; hoping to gain strength and courage from David's cries to the Lord.

I was preparing myself for battle. Strengthening my resolve. For months before I was removed from my parent's home, my father's defense team with the help of my mother, had persuaded me to refuse to testify.

They had convinced me that the staff I was waiting with, who are there to provide help and comfort to victims, were against me. So, I was steeling my resolve to do something I had never done: stand up to and defy authority.

After several moments of waiting, I asked Cat if she could ask if my mom was there. My mom had said she would meet us and I would see her before I took the stand. The prosecutor's staff said they had not seen her, but assumed she was with the defense, because Stan was already in the court room.

So, I waited to be called to stand.

After what seemed to be an eternity, they said they were ready. I didn't know how I was going to walk down the street from the prosecutor's office to the court room. My legs were trembling and I felt like my feet were made of cement.

I focused on only one thing. Putting one lead foot in front of the other. Although the July sun continued to beat down, I shivered. My brain felt like static on a television. Other than the immense size of the courthouse, I didn't take in any other details of its outer appearance as the ground held my eyes.

At this point there was no way out, only through.

We went in a back door and walked through winding hallways that felt as though they'd never end - until we finally reached those massive wooden double doors.

I had never seen or been in a courtroom before – other than on TV.. The room was large, cavernous. And everything inside looked as though they had been placed there hundreds of years ago. The type of room I imagined the Founding Fathers signed the Constitution in. Every empty surface was framed by thick wooden beams with intricate carvings. I remember thinking that if under different circumstances, the room would have been a beautiful one to photograph.

Suddenly, the temperature swung from freezing cold to stifling heat. Was that my nerves or decades old A/C in a hundred-year-old building? Probably both.

The judge seemed like he was sitting on the peak of a mountain. On my left, the jury box was a blur of faces. In front of me was the state's attorney. He was a grumpy faced old man. I probably only thought this because due to my reluctance to testify, our interactions had not been friendly. Behind them, sat my foster mom, my foster sister and my two case workers.

I felt like Goldilocks when she sat down in papa bear's chair. The chair and the room were huge in comparison to my meek self.

On the right side of the room sat Stan's attorney, who had been happy to coach me and be friendly behind the scenes, but on this day was eerily silent, without even a smile of encouragement. And Stan, of course, who was wearing a blue suit and coordinating tie. The only person behind them was my mother. I watched as she leaned forward and squeezed his shoulder in support as I took the stand.

I was sworn in and asked to scoot closer to the mic as my small voice murmured, "I plead the fifth. I reserve my right to remain silent." Over and over, I repeated this as the prosecutor became visibly frustrated.

He asked the judge to order me to answer. I refused. The judge explained to me that refusing to answer questions would put me in contempt of court. The judge then explained if I were held in contempt, I would be arrested and sent to juvenile detention for 30 days. Then, we would begin the process over again and would continue sending me to juvenile until I cooperated.

As an adult and a mother, I can't imagine watching this unfold. My heart breaks as I see my younger self on that stand. I can't imagine the feeling of agony if my child was up there. How did my parents just sit by and watch the turmoil and terror on my face?

The judge called a brief recess and had one of the paralegals explain to me that if I wanted, I could call my own council. That if I asked, I could have a public defender come speak to me and advise me of my next steps.

For the first time that day, I breathed and said, "Your Honor, I'd like to request a council of my own." and finally someone came to be on *my* side.

I was taken to a small conference room to wait for the arrival of my attorney. I was alone for what felt like another eternity but was a matter of minutes.

I asked again for my mom and this was when I was informed that since she came in with and remained on the side of the defense, I would not be allowed to see her until after I testified.

They allowed Cat to come in and bring me some water. But I mostly waited alone. After a while, a young, friendly looking man came in and introduced himself. Unfortunately, I don't remember his name. And honestly, not much of our conversation either. I know he asked if my earlier statements were true and if I had told the truth about what my dad did to me.

I replied that it was the truth. I explained to him that I didn't want to testify because I didn't want to be the one to destroy my family. I didn't want to be the one who sent my dad to jail and ruin everyone's lives.

I only told because I didn't want him to hurt me anymore.

He took out his wallet, and inside was a picture of two young, pretty girls; his daughters. He asked what I would do to protect them. He asked, if they were me, what would I want someone to do? So, I said "tell the truth." He asked "to take the person doing bad out of their lives? "Of course," I said in a trembling voice." He said, "do it for them."

So, I took a deep, shuddering breath. He promised he would be right behind me.

The air was tense as I walked back into the room. I felt as if I was walking the plank on Captain Hook's ship. I didn't feel like a hero or a warrior walking to deliver the finishing blow of victory. But more like Judas kissing the cheek of Jesus before his crucifixion.

The prosecutor began gently by asking me to identify Stan and what he was wearing. The prosecutor then proceeded to lead me through Stan's confession by first confirming the technical and legal terms of body parts and actions. Never in my life had I spoken the words for "penis" or "vagina." Now, I was referring to mine in a room full of adults that included my own parents.

We went through confirming the vague details of Stan's confession. Then the prosecutor took a deep breath and began to ask for as many details as I could recall.

The locations - every home we had lived in across the states of Missouri and Ohio as well as my grandparent's homes.

The frequency - every night the door creaking open and Stan sneaking in. Every time Stan pulled back the shower curtain and peered at my small, innocent, developing body. Whenever we were alone in a vehicle.

And finally, worst of all, the details of the acts themselves. What Stan used to violate me. I felt myself go cold and it became harder to catch my breath as I detailed his mouth, his fingers, and one terrifying time, what I guessed from the way it felt, a cold unsharpened pencil. My mom was silently crying. Shoulders shaking, head down. Stan sat stoically at the table, hands folded. He showed no emotion as I proceeded to answer each question. He stared at his hands and the table as I spoke each agonizing detail. The words felt like shards of glass falling from my tongue, shredding me from the inside as I bared my soul to strangers.

I could have been on the stand for a minute or an hour, I honestly don't recall. It felt like both the shortest and longest moment of my life. All I knew is I wanted it over. I wanted nothing more than to see Levi and feel the safety of my head on his shoulder.

I watched Stan's attorney's face tighten in a silent plea for me to stick to the script we had agreed on several months before.

I did my best to hold in the tears and reminded myself what my foster dad had told me that morning. "Head high, shoulders back. Don't let 'em see you sweat." I walked off the stand once again on trembling legs.

My brother testified next, but I am unaware for how long. He was so young too, 13. I believe his testimony was mostly incoherent from his tears. It was only after Bobby came off the stand that I finally had contact with my mom. Her face was hard, tear soaked. She kept pushing us in front of her. Saying "go, just let's get out of here," out of earshot from anyone else. The hallway was unending. We finally reached an alcove of vending machines.

My mom whirled around to face me. My heart had long ago stopped beating. I could feel bile in the back of my throat. "How could you? You promised!" My brother piled on, "you promised. How could you turn your back on our family?" And my mother again, "He's gone now, they will send him away. What are we going to do? Alice, how could you?"

I could only muster a whisper, although everything inside me was screaming.

"I told the truth."

Chapter 38

A Letter to My Mom

Mom,

I'm sure this letter will be as equally hard to read as it is to write. However, it is time for both to be done. This isn't about whether I love you, because the fact is, I do love you. But I am angry. The purpose of this letter is not to hurt you, though it will. Or to anger you, though it will. I would like to say it's about seeking answers, though I don't think there are any. And I've learned that truth over time becomes distorted to opinion.

It has been 20 years since my life changed forever. 20 years since my idea of safety, wellbeing, and yes, innocence was shattered. I don't blame you for Stan's actions and decisions. I write this letter only to say that for seven years and countless hours, I endured, dealt with, and lived through everything he did to me. Because as a child, I thought I had to protect you and Bobby. From whatever consequences, shame, and ridicule would come from my confessing. I don't know the explanations or excuses Stan gave you, or when they came. I do know that in his mind he holds me accountable. Not as a victim, but as some "co-conspirator." Maybe you feel the same way, or maybe you don't. Either way, I feel it needs to be said. I was a child. I was your child. Through every bit of it. Through each instance of abuse, through all the chaos, moving out at 16, going into foster care, enduring the trial, all of it. I was just a child.

Do you remember when you came to see me at Carol and Mike's house? You asked me, a 16-year-old child, YOUR 16-year-old child, who had just come forward with a lifetime's worth of pain and shame. "What do you want me to do? Do you want me to leave him?."

Still to this day, and even more especially now that I am a mother, this memory stops me cold and rips the air from my lungs. Whether you had ever known before of the abuse or not. You did then. You did on that day. And you chose Stan.

You left me, alone and scared, knowing what he had done. With nothing to my name. My mother left me on the porch and went home to my abuser.

You should have held me, apologized. Promised that he would never hurt me again. That you would rain down the fires of hell on him. That you would never leave me. That he would pay for hurting me. I was your angel, your baby.

Instead, you left me on the porch. And you went home. To Stan. To his bed. And I was alone, to cry myself to sleep. To wonder what had I done to deserve this? Was I such a bad girl? Wouldn't it just be better if I were dead?

I am not saying that you didn't have every right to be scared and angry. Or that you didn't have a right to grieve. Because I know you suffered a great loss as well.

I am saying that despite my age, my intelligence, or maturity, I was still a child. And maybe if that were the only time you chose him, it could be said it was a lapse in judgement, a result of shock or grief. But you kept choosing him, defending him. You stood by your man every single time.

In July, I met with the Victim's Advocate in Ohio. It was a long time coming. I had requested the transcripts of the trial. They were not stored properly, so they were gone. They did have Stan's confession. Also notes where you had met and cooperated with his attorney proving that you were always with him. Speaking to the Advocate confirmed so much for me such as how unnatural the situation was for a mother to abandon her child in favor of the perpetrator, how mishandled the case was by the prosecutor and Stan's attorney, and just how alone I really was at the time.

I will never forget how at the trial I sat on the stand all alone with only strangers on my side. I remember crying for you, wanting to see you. They told me I couldn't because you were with Stan. You were there to support Stan. I also remember coming off the stand to be confronted by your anger over my broken promise to not testify. How I was sending Stan to prison? Because he deserved prison.

Even before the trial, you let my brother and I be taken by strangers because you refused to separate from him. It was easier to send me away then to live without him. Why? What went through your mind, that it was easier for me to move out at 16, than to leave him?

As I've grown older and became not only a mother, but a wife, I must ask, how did you not know? All those years. How did you not question his behavior, or more importantly my behavior?

At your sister Patricia's funeral, the family bombarded me with demands that I forgive you. And I can let that go on their behalf, because all these years later they still have no idea what happened. Nor can they even understand. They see and feel a rift in their family and want to heal it as quickly as possible. How can you say you don't know what you've done but you're sorry? Sorry doesn't matter if you don't acknowledge your actions.

I have lived my whole adult life feeling like I am the one in the wrong. That I should be over this. But here is the thing. I was a child. Who I am has forever been shaped by, not only my father's abuse, but also by the aftermath of my confession of that abuse.

You and Stan were my parents. I didn't and don't expect perfection. I am a parent. I now know how hard it is. I also know that if this were my son, Leo, someone would have to kill me first. No matter how old he is!

Leo is almost the age I was at my first memory of abuse. I have been told that other's suspect it was happening when I was much younger. And I cannot fathom any of it.

Have you ever considered what carrying this felt like? Have you ever put yourself back in that front yard from my perspective? On the stand? In the basement of a foster home?

I understand if this seems selfish. But I have looked at it from your side. I have defended your position.

That he was the love of your life, the bread winner of our family. I have used the reasoning that Stan was mean and manipulative. I've tried to imagine having my child removed from me.

I believe you were hurt and broken.

But I was your child.

I have always said you don't know how you will handle a situation until you are in it. I am sure that is true about most things, but not this.

I have searched my soul to try to find a suitable reason. For the perfect answer to why you would turn from your child to the lowest form of man on earth.

I have spoken to professionals, friends and even strangers. I never wanted to act rashly. But after all these years, I have come to find that my thoughts were valid and that my feelings are real.

When you made these choices, you not only turned your back to me, but also to my children. I wanted to give you the opportunity to be a better grandmother than you were a mother. But I began to see the same choices, the same behaviors. Children are not accessories. We are souls; to be loved, protected, and cherished.

Still after all the pain, I watched you choose men over my child. Over me.

I can't allow that. I can't stand by while Leo is put in harm's way. Either physically or spiritually.

I have tried to move forward. To continue to share my life with you. But unfortunately, now when the tender moments come they only serve to shine a light on the times I was left alone.

I have had to navigate through the trauma, through becoming a woman, a wife, and a mother on my own and I have done that. I am who I am not because of the path life led me down, but despite it.

I do love you. For better or worse. But I am closing this chapter. I do not know what the next chapter holds or what role you will play in it, if any, if I am being honest.

I do hope that this letter leads you to search your own soul and find healing for yourself.

Alice

Chapter 39

Summer began to end, as did my relationship with Levi. I began to search for my own voice and identity. I began to act out in small ways. I chopped off my long, curly hair into a short and spiky pixie cut. Jennifer and I finally had a sisterly moment of bonding after months of utter disdain for one another.

Jennifer was getting her own apartment through an independent living program for foster kids. She would be moving out in just a few weeks. I knocked on the open-door frame between her room and mine while she was packing and said "Please don't throw anything at me, I come in peace.... with eye liner!"

Jennifer was an expert at dark, goth girl, winged eye liner. And that was the complete opposite of who I was. She looked up with mild curiosity and major annoyance. I spoke quickly "I want to look different from how I look everyday" to which she muttered under her breath "Like Glinda, the good witch."

"Yes, exactly. Will you help me?" I pleaded.

I was rewarded with a smile and she said, "I have been dying to."

We spent hours that evening bonding and doing my makeup. By the time we were done I thought to myself that I just might miss her a little bit.

I emerged from downstairs eager to show off my new makeover. My brother laughed, Ron just shook his head and smiled, and Cat said, "Good for you!"

I began to stretch my wings in tiny ways. I began to embrace things that seemed normal to most teenage girls but had been taboo for most of my life due to our religious beliefs. I experimented with makeup and hair color. I began listening to rock and hip-hop music. I even gave myself multiple ear piercings. I got into a little trouble for that because I got blood on Cat's decorative hand towels.

I had survived my dad's trial and was patiently waiting for the sentencing. After giving my testimony, there was no case left for his attorney to argue. They had based their whole defense on the premise of my commitment not to testify. When I did, it blew their case out of the water. They had not prepared any other recourse. I didn't get to hear the jury find him guilty because he accepted a plea bargain. His plea bargain was that he would plead "No Contest," meaning he was not admitting to guilt or proclaiming innocence, he accepted a six-year sentence in a minimum-security facility and would end up serving four years.

I knew that the only way I could go home before my eighteenth birthday was if my dad went to prison. However, in the way of most legal battles, his attorney played the game of continuances very well. Once a court date was on the docket, my dad's attorney would file a continuance, citing some type of scheduling conflict, illness, or other excuse.

One evening my mom called me. I was suspicious before I even answered the phone. Usually, I was always the one to initiate phone calls, especially in the evenings when my dad was home. My mom asked me if I would go somewhere where I could have a private conversation. I walked up the hill to Ron's garage and sat on a stump. Within a few moments, I heard the deep rumble of my father's voice.

There was no kind hello or any other niceties. He started the conversation by saying "I am not mad at you for testifying. That was a lot of pressure to stand strong against."

I let out a small chuckle and said, "I didn't buckle under pressure; I made my own choice."

His reply was "I am sure that's what they convinced you of, anyway."

I was not yet brave enough to continue to argue with him, so I just remained quiet. Hopeful that if I didn't say anything he would say what he needed to and we could move on. He tried for a few more minutes to provoke some type of response from me but as I had hoped by still being aloof, he moved on with his purpose for calling.

I sat quietly digging in the dirt with a stick I had found, listening to my father speak. My father was a master at manipulation. I remember when I was little hearing people say that he could sell ice to penguins or combs to bald men. He just had a way with words. No matter how confident you were in what you felt or believed in, he would always find a way to sway you and change your mind to his way of thinking. And he did it so adeptly that most of the time you would be hours away from the conversation before you realized it happened.

My dad continued to say that although he wasn't upset by my choice to testify it did mean that there would be some direct and intense changes for the family. I bit my tongue on the retort that we were currently in foster care and wards of the state, therefore we were not at the moment "a family." I knew that being snarky would only deepen and prolong the conversation.

My dad explained to me how his plea bargain worked and what to expect from the sentencing hearing. I asked when he thought sentencing would be and he said that normally sentencing would occur seventy-five to ninety days after trial. That would put us in the vicinity of October. However, his attorney hoped that by putting in a request of continuance for personal reasons, they could push it out until November.

At that I did find my voice. "Why so long?" What I didn't say out loud is that if he wasn't sentenced and in prison, I was stuck in foster care. To answer my question my dad said simply, "So you can be there."

Why did I need to be there? I thought to myself. Dad let me sit in silence for a moment before saying, "I thought that you could give a victim's impact statement. You can write a letter and tell the judge that you want to see your family made whole. That you want to have us back together and pursue a path to healing. Also, that we cannot pursue that path if I am in prison."

I listened to the buzz of the cell phone connection and looked up at the darkening sky. I let my breath leak out of me slowly. I was so weary. I just wanted everything to be over.

If someone asked me what "over" meant or looked like, I couldn't tell you. I didn't know. All I did know is that I wanted to be far away from where I currently was.

After a moment, I heard my mom say quietly "Please don't be selfish, think of me and your brother. He still has several years before he is grown. He needs your dad home."

I told them both I would think about it. My dad even encouraged me to pray about it, to which I replied, "I'm not doing much praying lately."

I hung up and walked slowly back down the driveway, dragging my feet, and kicking rocks the whole way. I knew if Ron saw me he would say "Why are you kicking my rocks, little girl?" But he was working late and not in his garage.

I walked in the house and down to the basement. I was ready for an argument. I headed straight for Jennifer's room, but she was out shopping for her new apartment.

I laid down in the middle of the basement floor and stared at the ceiling. There was no one to argue with and my tears were spent. I was screaming inside for someone to look for me, to notice the turmoil, to recognize my despair.

But once again, no one did.

Chapter 40

If there ever was a montage music moment in the movie of my life, my summer in foster care would be it. There were good days and there were terrible days. Mostly there were just days stacked on top of each other.

I continued to be insistent about wanting to go home and my case workers continued to be consistent in their avoidance of the subject. I also began to question why we had to have supervised visits. I didn't understand why we couldn't just go to my mom's apartment.

It was time for Connie's monthly visit. For the most part when Connie came, I simply ignored her. Connie would come in and say, "I need to at least see you and your brother's faces." I would stand in front of her, do a twirl, fake a smile, and walk away, throwing a snarky "bye, Connie" over my shoulder.

But this month, I was going to confront her. I had asked Cat if she would ask on my behalf when we could start unsupervised visits. But she said she wasn't going to speak for me anymore. If I had questions, I was old enough to ask them myself.

I was sitting on the back deck reading a book when Connie peeked her head out of the balcony doors and said, "Cat said you had some questions for me?" I blurted out "Why are my visits with my mom still supervised?" Connie could see that I was preparing myself for an argument, so she replied in her no-nonsense tone that "unsupervised visits were not recommended at this time." And if that was all I wanted to discuss, she had to leave to attend her next visit. Then Connie left. No other explanation, no argument.

I was angry. I had finally gotten up the courage to try to speak on my own behalf and seek information about my own case. I wasn't a little kid. I had opinions and questions. I was seventeen. I was old enough to have some input and knowledge as to what was happening in my own environment. I just wanted to be heard.

There were so many adults in charge of me and my life. Most of these adults had only read about me on paper. The few that did take time to speak to me always seemed to have an agenda. I was desperate for an adult I could speak to that was caring, yet unbiased. Someone that would hear my questions and desires. As an adult, I know that those requests may not have been healthy or safe, because I wasn't able to comprehend my situation with the maturity and clarity of an adult. However, I believe that my concerns and desires deserved to be heard.

Throughout my journey to healing, one of my most important goals is "to be the person I needed." One way I have found to carry out that mission is to volunteer with my local CASA program.

The Court Appointed Special Advocates is a program designed specifically to allow children access to special volunteers. These volunteers are trained to be unbiased voices for children who are neglected and abused and often go unheard or fall through the cracks of the family protection system.

CASA is the only program where volunteers are appointed as officers of the court by the judge to represent a child's best interest.

The CASA program's beginning was inspired in 1976 in Seattle when juvenile court Judge David Soukup realized he did not have sufficient information to make a life changing decision in the case of a three-year-old girl who had suffered from abuse. Judge Soukup realized that there was no one in the court room to speak solely on the child's behalf with no other agenda to keep or goals to be met. The judge had his bailiff contact a few people in the community to bring a sack lunch to the juvenile court to discuss ideas. Fifty people showed up for that brown bag lunch meeting and from that meeting the CASA program was born.

A CASA works with legal and child welfare professionals, educators, and service providers to ensure that judges have all the information needed to make a well-rounded decision on behalf of the child. Volunteers build relationships with the child and parents as well as the child's placement and stay involved in the case until it is closed and a suitable resolution is made on the child's behalf.

As of this writing, there are 950 CASA programs spread out over forty-nine states. There are over 400,000 children aged 0-21 in foster care in the United States on any given day and more than 85,000 CASA volunteers. There are 242,236 children being served by CASA nationwide. Children with a CASA volunteer are half as likely to spend time in long-term foster care.

Cases involving CASA's are more likely to be permanently closed with fewer than 10 percent re-entering the foster care system. CASA's generally only carry one or two cases ensuring that each child gets unbiased, consistent, and caring personal attention.

The impact that a volunteer would have made in my life would have been incredible. I would have been able to have someone who was willing to share the truth of the case and details with me. That would have helped to combat so much of the confusion and manipulation that my parents used against me behind the scenes. I also would have had a better understanding of what lay ahead after I turned eighteen and aged out of foster care.

Chapter 41

Connie wouldn't give me answers. Cat did not have the answers. My mom avoided the questions and there was no CASA on the case for me to turn to. Once again I was alone with no adult to look to with my questions and fears. I just wanted to know what was going on. I wanted to know what the plan was and what the next steps needed to be.

I finally turned to Rachel, my agency caseworker. Rachel took me out for pancakes. It was a rare visit between us without my brother. I began to pour my heart out to her and I felt her frustration begin to rise. My words trailed off as I saw Rachel begin to shake her head. She looked me in the eye and said "If no one else is going to tell you, I will. You deserve to know the truth."

I looked at her quizzically. "The truth about what?"

"The truth about your mom."

At this point in the summer, visits were allowed to be held anywhere and at any time through the day, as long as Cat could supervise them. This included Ron and Cat's home. My mom was working as an assistant manager at a local dollar store. I knew she worked a lot of hours because she was only able to visit us once a week for about half an hour or so. That was why I wanted to be allowed to have visits at her apartment. I thought if we had the freedom of unsupervised visits, I would be able to see her more because it would better fit her schedule.

Rachel blurted out, "Your mother has been seen with your father. Before you argue or defend her, just know, she has been seen several times by a reliable source."

I demanded, "Who?" Rachel lowered her eyes and said "Me, Alice. I live in the same area that your mom lives and works. I personally have seen your parents together. At the grocery store, out to dinner, and several times in the car together. Also, Connie has caught him sneaking out of the apartment as she was showing up for a visit with your mom."

I felt like someone had kicked me in the stomach. I knew that Rachel wouldn't lie to me but I couldn't wrap my heart around the truth. How could she? How could my mom betray me and my brother? The plan was so simple. All she had to do was not talk to my father, not see my father. I couldn't understand. I knew she was lonely and scared. But if she would just stay away from him, I could come home and she wouldn't be alone.

At this point in my life, I hadn't even processed the fact that my mom up to this point had chosen to stay with a man who had molested her daughter. The situation was straightforward. My mother's children could be returned to her custody and care *if* she maintained no contact with the man who molested their daughter. That was it. I knew in my heart that she had made a choice. My mother made the choice every day to continue in her marriage with the man who abused me in one of the most wicked manners.

I asked Rachel if we could go home. I just wanted to crawl back into my bed. I wasn't sure how to process the information spoken to me. My brain kept trying to rationalize her actions; to come up with excuses and justifications.

It all made sense though. The way my mom hurried off the phone or could only stay for a few minutes at a time, especially if visits were in the evening. The way she always parked in the next parking lot and walked over to us when we were meeting in public. She couldn't stand to be away from him, so he would literally ride with her and wait in the car during our visits. As the loose ends began to tie themselves, I was stunned. I couldn't even cry.

My first thought was to confront my mother. I wanted to berate her. I wanted to list all the ways that she had failed, neglected, and abandoned me. But I knew that to argue with her would only confound the situation. My mom had a way of twisting evidence against her to instead make herself look like the victim.

I felt like I was banging my head against a wall. I was trying every way I could to advocate for myself, my brother, and even my mother. I was doing everything I could to get us home. Yet, she couldn't even do the most basic step. It was hopeless.

As it turns out, I wouldn't have the opportunity to confront my mother even if I wanted to as we were headed out as a whole family to visit Ron's family in Tennessee for the weekend. Ron was raised by his aunt and uncle, who owned a car lot in a tiny town, and they were hosting a festival at their lot for the community. So, we all went down to help. Cat was at a conference in Texas and would be meeting us later in the weekend.

We loaded up in the SUV. Jenn, my brother, Morgan, myself, and Ron. The trip had a very rough start. Jennifer had threatened to "squash me like a soda can" over seating arrangements before we were even loaded in the vehicle. I did not have the will to fight with her. I simply rolled my eyes and said "Jennifer! I don't care where I sit. I will ride on the luggage rack on top of the car if you just shut up and leave me alone." I climbed into the middle seat between Morgan and my brother, opened my book and stayed quiet throughout the six-hour drive. My goal for the weekend was to just stay out of Jennifer's way. I had my book, minutes on my cell phone, and my disposable camera. I would be fine.

Jennifer was in my face at every opportunity that weekend. The more I ignored or avoided her, the more Jenn was angered. By the end of the second day, I was worn thin. I was tired and sad. Despite being angry with her, I just wanted to talk to my mom. I tried calling her, but there was no answer. I thought maybe she was at work; I would wait until her store closed and try again.

Ron's aunt had offered to pay me if I would help that weekend with filing and other small clerical jobs around the car lot's office. I spent the day finishing the filing and some cleaning. Around 9 p.m. that night, I tried to call my mom again. Still no answer.

I finally broke down. I could no longer mask or bottle up my emotions. I called Cat and like a shaken-up bottle of soda left in the sun all day, I spewed everything to Cat before she could even say hello. I told her all about Rachel catching my mom with my dad, Jennifer picking on me, and my mom not answering her phone. I told her I just didn't want to be here anymore, and I didn't have any solutions. I even considered just grabbing my bag and leaving. I didn't have anywhere to go or any knowledge on how to survive on my own. I just wanted out. After about fifteen minutes, Cat finally calmed me down. She told me she was about four hours away and that I should go lay down and try to rest. She told me that I could ride with her on the way home, just the two of us. That was enough to comfort and calm me. But I still didn't know what was going on with my mom.

The next morning, Cat confronted Jennifer and told her she needed to leave me alone. We finished the weekend and headed home. I had been gone for five days; I had tried calling my mom more times than I could count. She had not answered once.

We were back in Ohio for two days before my mom finally called. She didn't call me, she called Cat, and asked about visiting. Cat said she could come but warned her that I was pretty upset. Later that evening, my mom pulled up the long driveway while I sat on the porch.

My mom sat down beside me and asked how my trip was. I told her it sucked. She tried to make small talk, but I had nothing to say to her. After ten minutes she stood up and said, "If you are only going to give me attitude, I am not going to stay." I laughed. That's all I could do. And she did. My mom left.

We didn't talk for two weeks. She would visit my brother. But I just couldn't face her. I eventually gave in. I decided I had to try, so once again I put my feelings aside and reconciled with her.

As a peace offering, my mom had the pictures from my Tennessee trip developed for me. When she brought them to me, I was excitedly shuffling through them, showing my mom the good parts of my trip.

Then I came across a picture of my mom. She was sitting on a large piece of driftwood in a blue dress, with a huge lake behind her.

I said "You look very pretty. When was this?"

She said "Oh. I went away while you were gone."

"Oh."

I continued shuffling through the pictures, the next one was a light house on one of the great lakes of Michigan, the next one was of my dad sitting on the same piece of driftwood. My mom must have turned in her film at the same time she turned in mine and both sets ended up in my envelope at the store.

I felt the air whoosh out of my lungs. I simply stared up at her. My mom began to search around for an explanation, but she was caught.

She knew there was no explanation that would make sense. So, she just told me the truth.

My mom said that she thought since we were in Tennessee it would be a suitable time for her to get away. She had always wanted to see a light house. But mostly she wanted good memories with my dad before he went to prison.

My mom said that the last year had brought strain to her marriage but in some ways had helped them renew their love for each other because they had time to focus on their marriage while my brother and I had been away in foster care. They went to the light house to renew their commitment to each other and celebrate how they had endured through all that life had thrown at them.

I quietly asked her "Do you not want us to come home?" Her answer was this: "Of course I want you to come home. You will be coming home on your birthday regardless of what happens. And once your dad is sentenced and they take him away, Bobby will be able to come home shortly after. Your dad will be gone for a long time, at least a few years. I just want to make the most of the time I have with him."

I handed her the pictures and walked inside. I said nothing because there was nothing to say. I didn't know how to process the blatant betrayal and abandonment. All those calls that went unanswered while I was in Tennessee were because she was on a second honeymoon with the man who molested me. The man whose presence in her home kept her children in a stranger's home. This was in July. I had three more months to go.

Chapter 42

I woke up the next morning with a new resolve. I had to figure out what I was going to do when October came. I began to ask questions of Cat, Rachel, and Connie.

I still wanted to go home, although, if I was honest with myself, I wasn't sure why. Home had never been a safe place for me. It wasn't a place filled with love and honesty. But it was all I had ever known. I felt like Dorothy when she clicked her heels together to leave Oz. She was so set on getting home, she hadn't considered the damage the tornado did when she left. I was very much the same way. I had spent all my time trying to convince everyone around me to send me home, I didn't stop to think about what that actually meant.

We had never been without my father, so that was unimaginable. And although on the surface I was angry with my mother for all the instances of betrayal, my heart remained in denial.

I imagined a place where my mom, my brother, and I would live in peace. A place where we would work together to survive and build a new life. A place out from under my father's thumb.

But that was never to be our reality.

I also imagined that I would wake up on my eighteenth birthday, as an adult, with all the hidden adult knowledge and confidence. I would get a job and a place of my own and figure out what life had in store for me.

That too was not reality. I could barely order my own food or ask for a packet of ketchup at a fast-food restaurant due to my shyness and crippling anxiety. There was no way I could manage a job. I didn't have the first clue how to function on a social or professional level.

So, how do we solve the problem of my future? Where was I going to go?

The first person I went to was Rachel, my foster agency case worker. I had always been fond of her, but we had grown even closer since her revelation about my mother. Although there had been some strain of late with me holding the secret of my parent's "honeymoon" and the phone call from my dad. I still trusted Rachel and felt like I could honestly express my concerns to her.

The first thing she did was encourage me to begin looking for a job. It could be part time and since I wasn't reliant on the paycheck yet, it could be somewhere I liked or might consider fun. We began by learning how to dress appropriately to look for a job and then went around and simply asked for applications. This alone was a huge step for me.

On the way home, Rachel and I began to discuss the possibility of me joining the independent living program. Independent living was a voluntary program for teenagers, starting as early as age fourteen, who would be aging out of the foster care system. The program supplied many avenues of support including academic support, help finding a job, budgeting and financial management, and other life skills needed to survive successfully as an adult. At the end of your completion of the program, and leading up to your emancipation from foster care, you would be assigned an apartment and given financial aid to help you learn to live on your own as an adult. While living in the apartment you would have to follow certain rules and standards, such as keeping a job, continuing your education, remaining alcohol, and drug free, as well as keeping your home clean and livable.

The program is an amazing asset to many teenagers aging out of the foster care system. I wanted to take part, however there were a few obstacles standing in my way. The first was time. I was just a couple of months away from my eighteenth birthday, there simply wasn't enough time for me to complete the needed classes. Also, one of the main requirements of the program was to be in school with passing grades or pursuing a GED. I had not attended school since the sixth grade, I had stopped pursuing my homeschool curriculum a couple of years after that. I did not have the emotional strength or the educational foundation to be put into a traditional high school setting.

Rachel agreed to gather more information and see if there were any exemptions or options available to me, but this didn't seem like a likely solution.

Cat and I sat at the small dinette filling out the applications I had gathered. I didn't even know my own social security number. It quickly began to dawn on me how ill prepared I was for the next stage of my life. I didn't have the faintest clue what the next step would look like. It was like trying to look out a window without being able to push the curtain aside.

I could tell that Cat was becoming visibly concerned. It was just now starting to sink in for myself and everyone around me that it wasn't about preparation, but capability.

Connie came for a visit a few days later and we approached her asking for ideas that could help me. Her first question was what I imagined would happen when I turned eighteen. I told her I didn't know. My whole life up to that point had been directed by my parents and their religion. I didn't know how to make choices for myself. Connie asked if any of my family members would be willing to let me move back in with them. I simply shrugged.

I didn't know. Our family had rallied around us in the beginning of our removal, but after a few weeks their communication with us began to wane and eventually die off. I suppose my mom kept them updated on our well-being and the progression of the case. But that meant that my extended family only knew what my mom decided to tell them.

For the last several months, I was once again isolated. I had my foster family and visits with my mom continued to be on a weekly basis. All visits were still supervised and noticeably short. I would see my mom for about forty-five minutes a week and speak to her on the phone for about fifteen minutes a day.

No one had reached out to me to check in, to directly ask about my well-being. No one had come to my dad's trial. No one offered for me to come and stay after I had to leave Cat and Ron's.

I knew that my mom expected me to come home to her and that weighed heavily on me as well. I felt an incredible amount of pressure to please and obey her. I didn't know how to think for myself or how to take care of myself.

Cat and Ron offered for me to stay at their house. They said they would teach me to drive, help me get a car, and a job. They would teach me how to take care of myself. Cat promised she would find out what we would need to do for that to happen. We would learn that having me remain in their home after my emancipation wasn't allowed and would affect their foster license.

I only had one choice: to return home to my mother's apartment after my eighteenth birthday.

Chapter 43

The rest of August passed in a hazy blur. I had settled into a restless contentment. I passed the time reading and swimming in the pool. By far, the best part of my summer took place in the pool in the backyard. It was a small four foot deep above ground pool, but it brought me vast amounts of joy and distraction over those summer weeks. We had never had unrestricted access to a pool before so it felt like we had hit the jackpot.

As September began, the leaves fell and my foster siblings went back to school. The house was once again quiet during the day. I knew my time in Cat and Ron's home was drawing to its inevitable close. I was finally going home. My little brother would be staying, however. It had become clear that there would be no opportunity for him to come home unless, and until, our dad was incarcerated.

We were all aware that my mom continued to have regular contact with my dad, but only I knew that he had officially been living in the apartment with my mom for several weeks. I am not sure how soon after our removal he moved in with her, but she wasn't on her own for awfully long.

I couldn't imagine moving back home and sharing a living space with him. But I was at a loss as to where to go. My foster family couldn't keep me. I wasn't eligible for any assistance from my foster agency or the state of Ohio. I hadn't heard from any of my relatives. Levi's family had been my refuge through all of this, but since we had broken up, I had lost contact with those in his family to which I was close.

When I would speak to the adults in my life, such as my case workers and my therapist, they all told me the same thing: I needed to decide for myself.

However, I was incapable of making my own decisions. I was frozen, paralyzed. I didn't know how to move forward or where to go. If I didn't go home to my mom, where would I go? We were in a very rural community. There weren't shelters or any programs for homeless young adults. And even if there had been, I couldn't fathom how to survive on my own. I was legally an adult, but in so many ways I was still a child.

The reality that I was going home was beginning to sink in. I had spent so much time fighting against everyone to try to get there, that I didn't even consider what that meant. From the day we were removed, the removal itself, and those who removed us became the enemy. The reason we were removed has somehow gotten swept under the rug. It was so easy for everyone to focus on that shared trauma that the real trauma seemed to be forgotten. Especially by my mother. With every opportunity, my parents rallied us around the common enemy of "them." The state, the caseworkers, the prosecutor, and the judge. They were all just out to keep us apart. My dad expertly stoked the fires of our collective anger so that we turned towards anyone but him.

I had spent all my life trying to be obedient and pleasing to my parents. I had learned in early childhood how to mask my feelings, fears, and even my needs to keep peace in our home. The less attention I needed, the more praise I received. I had spent all seventeen years of my life trying to please and appease my parents. This situation was no different. Their wishes were quite literally my commands. I had to go home. There were no other options.

In the last few weeks, I had reconnected with a friend from Missouri. Daniel and I had been friends since I was fourteen and even dated sporadically despite the distance between us. He had reached out to my mom by phone and she begrudgingly filled him in on the basics of what had happened while we had been out of contact with each other. With a lot of convincing on his part, she gave him my cell phone number and we had spent the last few weeks talking to each other and catching up.

Danny had just turned twenty and was looking for a change. He had a terrible relationship with his parents and wanted to get away for a while. I confided in him that I was lost. I had no clue what, where, or how to move to the next stage of my life. I was scared to go back to my parents, but I didn't know what else to do.

At first, I begged him to come and get me. I called him, crying in the middle of the night, begging him to please come pick me up. We could run away together, from both of our families, and start over. However, this was real life and not a romance novel. We had no money, no car, and nowhere to go. Danny said there was something he could do. He could come to me in Ohio. We knew my parents were not going to be in favor of this. But I knew that if Danny were with me when I moved into my mom's apartment, I would have protection. I would have someone on my side. Someone to take care of me. We decided to talk to my mom. I told her I was coming home on my eighteenth birthday to her small apartment. I wanted Danny to come up to Ohio and stay with us, I wanted a deadbolt lock on my bedroom door and a phone line installed.

If I had no choice but to go home, I would go home on my terms.

Chapter 44

The night before my eighteenth birthday was full of nervous energy for everyone. Ron and Cat took the family out to dinner at the same local diner we had went to on my first night at their house, to send me off the same way they welcomed me in. They did this even while knowing they would still see me on a regular basis, because my brother would be staying for a while longer.

After dinner, I began to pack up the belongings I had accumulated over my five-month stay. I was leaving with quite a bit more than I had come with. It was strange the way this journey in foster care had begun, surprising and abrupt. The end of the journey was planned but felt equally as abrupt.

In twenty-four hours, I would be back under the same roof as my parents. One who had abused me and one who had abandoned me. I was so wrapped up in making sure that everything was the way that everyone else wanted and needed the circumstances to play out that I didn't, and couldn't, process my own feelings. At this point, I was simply an object being pushed around by the current created by my parents.

My birthday dawned a bright and chilly October morning. For once in the last five months, my mom was on time. Danny loaded my bags in the trunk of my mom's tiny Geo Prizm while I hugged Cat and my brother goodbye.

Leaving my brother behind was hard even though I knew that it wasn't forever and I would be visiting him in a few days.

My mom and I were awkwardly polite with each other on the twenty-minute drive to her apartment. By the time we reached the highway and with each mile further away from Cat and Ron's I felt my confidence in my decision ebbing away and the doubts began to creep in. Although I was legally an adult, I felt myself falling backwards in time. Each mile closer to her home I felt myself shrink. In the last few months, especially after my breakup with Levi, I had begun to find myself and my own voice because I no longer had him to speak up for me.

All of that disappeared when I opened the front door of that small two-bedroom apartment. There he sat. My dad. I hadn't seen him since I sat opposite him in the courtroom. The air whooshed out of me like a punch to the gut. My mind went blank. My hands were cold and trembling. I wanted to turn and run. I knew if I ran, he would feel as if he had won. My dad didn't believe I had the guts to face him. I stood face to-face with the dragon. Would I back down and run, or would I stand my ground?

I crossed the threshold and said "Hi, Dad." I don't know what I expected. I wanted apologies and humbleness. I wanted my parents to say they realized they were wrong and we were all going to get help. I should have known better.

My dad smirked and said "Happy Birthday. I couldn't get a dead bolt on that door and we can't afford another phone line, so guess you will have to figure it out."

I looked him dead in the face and said "Don't worry. There will always be a butcher knife under my pillow."

I could feel him taunting me, challenging my strength and my bravery. My dad still loved to make me feel small.

I could feel the mockery in his tone and saw it in his smirk. I silently begged for my mom to see it; to step in and tell him to leave me alone. Instead, she let out a gasp as if shocked by my response. Danny cleared his throat in the awkward silence and said he was going to get my things from the car. I excused myself to use the restroom.

I sat down on the toilet lid and let myself tremble and breathe for a moment. I stood up and ran freezing water over my wrists to help ground myself. As I stared at myself in the tiny mirror above the sink, I knew that I had to take care of myself. No one believed that I could survive this. Everyone was waiting for me to fail. Once again there were so many opinions, but no solutions. I knew my dad expected me to wither in his presence, to automatically bend to his will, but I wasn't going to. And I wasn't going to run away either. I would show him that I belonged here. It wasn't a privilege. My mom owed me a safe place to stay until I could figure out how to take care of myself. They had let me down in every other way. I wasn't going to let them out of this. I was uncomfortable and scared. But if I had to feel this way, so would they.

I plastered a smile on my face. It would be an exceptionally long time before my mask would come off again. I walked back into the living room and said, "Hand me a beer, it's my birthday!"

Myself, Danny, my mom, and my dad would end up sharing a living space for almost two months before my dad went to prison. It was far from a "home" and we were far from functional.

I started drinking alcohol regularly with that first beer on my eighteenth birthday. Thus began a decade-long battle with alcohol. Drinking made me feel at peace. I felt bulletproof. I could finally say what was on my mind, and I did. But as good as it felt to voice my emotions, it also led to many arguments. It wasn't uncommon for me to start drinking as soon as my feet hit the floor in the morning. Many nights ended with me passed out laying in front of my bedroom door, barricading myself in with my own body. I could see the destruction. I could see myself drowning, but I couldn't stop. I had finally found something that assuaged and quenched the fire that was burning my soul.

My parents not only supplied the alcohol, but they participated in it. I honestly think it was the only way we could face each other.

Here is some context to how truly upside-down things were. I was eighteen, a legal adult. I drank with my parents daily. My twenty-year-old boyfriend was living with me and my parents. Despite all of this, my parents still expected Danny and I to abide by rules regarding our physical contact. It was a constant point of tension between Danny and I that I didn't stand up to them. We did have a physical relationship, but we were still sneaking around like kids. We didn't hold hands in public or snuggle on the couch.

It was so lopsided to have access to power but to not know how to use it. I was stuck again. I was eighteen. I could be on my own, doing what I wanted. I was sneaking into bars with my own mother but couldn't kiss my boyfriend goodnight.

My dad would find little ways like that to keep me under his power. It felt like those old shows on TV where they would hypnotize people and then with a certain trigger word, make them act like a chicken. It was just a look from my dad and I felt my resolve drain from me like the drain being pulled from a bathtub.

I don't have many of clear memories from those two months. It was a revolving door of waking up powerless and afraid, drinking to shut it out, and yelling at everyone. The four of us argued constantly. I argued with Danny. I argued with my parents. My parents argued with each other. It was a terribly toxic environment.

My dad went to prison in the beginning of December. Danny went home to Missouri for Christmas. My mom and I finally got to have an overnight visit with my brother. The three of us went back to Indiana for Christmas with my aunts and grandparents. I was sober for the first time in months. And I was miserable.

After the holidays, we returned to Ohio. My brother went back to Cat and Ron's. We still had a long way to go before he could come home even though our dad had gone to prison. Danny wouldn't be back until the first of the year. It was just my mom and me.

I thought that this would be the moment we had waited for. Healing would begin. We would bond and build a life. The two of us.

I couldn't have been more wrong. It was a nightmare. We both were still drinking heavily. We argued constantly. My mom felt as if I had ruined her life. She was grieving my dad. But she was also running around with men she would meet at the bar. For the first time in my life, I wasn't just emotionally and spiritually alone, I was physically alone.

After one particularly scary phone call in the middle of the night, Danny cut his visit short with his family. His dad drove him ten hours straight to get back to me. I was passed out on the sofa when he let himself into the apartment at four in the morning. He wrapped me in his arms and whispered that he had seriously doubted I would still be alive when he got there.

I knew something had to change. But I didn't know what to do. Danny's dad went to his hotel and left the two of us alone.

I wish I could say that Danny told me I needed to get sober and get help. But that wasn't quite the solution he came up with. As we sat on the couch watching a stupid action movie, he turned to me and said "Well, you want to get married and we can go back to Missouri with my dad?"

I said yes.

Chapter 45

Running away to another state to get married sounds so glamourous in the pages of romance novels. But in reality, it was awful. Don't get me wrong, I loved Danny, but I loved the idea of an escape even more.

My mom, my aunts, and my grandparents were furious. My aunt went as far as to tell me that by moving to Missouri, I was giving up my right to be a part of the family. That I was turning my back on them, so I should not expect them to run to my aid when everything fell apart. My whole life had been in shambles for the last two years and no one had come to my aid. They had bailed out my mom, but my brother and I had been left hanging in the balance. My aunt Nancy had all kinds of questions, mostly how would I take care of myself and why would I choose to throw away my future. Honestly, I wasn't even sure at this point if I had a future. I was doing the best I could to simply survive from one day to another.

Although Danny and I had been friends for many years, and dated off and on, even across the distance between Missouri and Ohio, I had never met his family more than in passing. So far I had spent a total of three days with my future father-in-law, and they were less than spectacular. He was not impressed with me, nor was I impressed of him. Richard was clear in his opinion of me. When we told him of our plans to come back to Missouri with him and get married, he responded by telling Danny that he was sure that I was an extremely sweet girl, but did he really want to spend the rest of his life with a ding bat? He asked this question with me sitting on the sofa right next to Danny. I was appalled. I had been called many things in my life, but stupid had never been one. I knew that Richard and Danny didn't have a great relationship. Richard was often emotionally and physically abusive to all four of his boys, but as Danny was the oldest, he withstood the worst of his father's anger. As an adult, Danny still struggled with trying to please his dad but constantly fell short.

Instead of arguing over whether I was indeed a ding bat, I left the room to give Danny a chance to talk to Richard. I returned to the conversation about an hour later and Richard had agreed to allow us to come back to and live with them. However, since they considered themselves to be a "good, Christian family," there would be a few stipulations. The first rule of course was that we could both live there but would have to sleep separately. The second was that Danny would have to get a job and I would have to do chores to help around the house. And the third rule was that within thirty days of moving in, we had to have a written five-year plan; including a budget. Again, I barely had the emotional strength to plan my outfit, let alone plan my life for the next five years. Nevertheless, we needed a place to go, so we agreed.

I remember one of the things my aunt said to try to convince me not to go was "What are you going to do when you start your period and have to ask for tampons?" She was referring to an instance when I was fourteen and we had gone on vacation with her, my uncle Bruce, and my grandparents to Florida. I started my period one day on the beach and was embarrassed to tell her and my Nanny. I told her I didn't know what I would do. I would have to figure it out. For the last two years everyone had been telling me it was time to grow up and learn to take care of myself. So that is what I was doing.

I packed up all I could. Honestly, I didn't have much. I had grown accustomed to moving around the last two years so I had learned to keep my belongings to a minimum of what would fit in a bag that I could carry by myself.

We set out on our ten-hour journey around 10 p.m. Despite being called a dingbat and our obvious differences, I was determined to make a good impression. I was also excited. I felt like I was in love and starting a new adventure, one that for once I had instigated. The trip started happily enough with the three if us singing to old eighties songs on the radio. We reached the Illinois state line by around 1 a.m. and decided to stop at a truck stop for breakfast. I went into the restroom and like a bad omen, like my aunt had sent it, I had started my period. I was mortified. I had one dollar bill in my pocket that I used in the machine hanging on the wall. I knew that it was only a temporary solution. I hoped that Danny's mom would be kinder and more open than his dad. It wasn't my first time dealing with this, despite my aunt's warning. Was it still embarrassing and awkward? Absolutely. But I had just recently been in foster care. I lived with complete strangers. I could handle this. Afterall, these people were supposed to be my new family, right?

I was quieter the rest of the trip as the reality began to sink in. We pulled in the driveway of my future in-laws home in the early hours of the morning. We were all exhausted, but I tried to rally and put on a happy face to meet my soon-to-be mother-in-law for the first time. Danny's mom, Susan, was up getting herself and Danny's brothers ready for the day. It had seemed as if Richard and I had bonded over the long drive and waffles, but upon entering the door, he demanded that I go to the kitchen and help Susan prepare biscuits from scratch. Danny, Susan, and I laughed and looked awkwardly at one another until it became clear that he wasn't joking. He began to tell a story of how when Susan was in labor with their youngest son he insisted she make him breakfast before he took her to the hospital. He went further to say that that was the kind of submissive wife that Danny also deserved and expected.

Ever the people-pleaser, I washed my hands and began to help mix the biscuits. This would become a rough start on a very rocky road.

Chapter 46

I thought running away and getting married was going to be a golden beginning. Getting married must be the missing piece that makes the whole puzzle fall in place. I was still naïve to how life worked. All the adults in my life seemed to know all the answers to life's inner workings. Since I didn't receive a secret wealth of knowledge on my eighteenth birthday, I thought getting married would be the key. We would say our vows, and then magically have a home of our own and a life that we controlled. Unfortunately, that is not how things worked out.

We had a date set for March. The weeks leading up to our wedding were fraught with drama. There were no dress fittings, cake tastings, bridal showers, or bachelor parties. There were daily arguments between Danny, Richard, and I.

One of those arguments between Danny and Richard escalated to Susan calling the police. Richard demanded we leave the house. They argued about us not having turned in our five-year plan. That is how it started, but that inevitably led to Richard berating Danny on how disrespected he felt. We had nowhere to go. It was the middle of the night in February. I waited for Susan to step in and be a voice of calm and reason to Richard as I was trying to be with Danny. However, she whispered to me to start dressing warm and grab as many blankets as I could. We ended up sleeping in the backseat of our 1977 Ford LTD, in his parent's driveway. Laying wrapped in blankets in the backseat of that ancient car, I realized there was no reprieve. This was not going to be the family that I had dreamed of and missed out on. I had jumped out of the frying pan and into the fire, as the saying goes.

Our first year of marriage was a roller coaster. We bounced back and forth between Danny's parents and grandparents. I was in a spiral of instability. I could barely make it through a day without a breakdown of some kind; usually at bedtime. I was easily overwhelmed by carrying around my past trauma and trying to overcome the daily challenges of being a wife and an adult. Danny tried to support me, but he was still young himself and was more interested in finally having freedom of adulthood. He wanted to hang out with his friends, drink beer, and smoke marijuana.

Nearing the end of our first year of marriage, I had reached my breaking point, so we made the first of many moves between Missouri and Indiana. We moved in with my mom and her then-boyfriend to the chorus of "I told you so" from everyone in my family. Living with my mom wasn't near as tumultuous or dramatic as Danny's parents, but nevertheless, it had its own difficulties. Having two other adults in the home afforded my mom the freedom to not be in the home. So, Danny and I were tasked with working and taking care of my now fifteen-year-old brother. It was like being given an instant family because it was left up to us to feed and manage an almost grown child as my mom divided her time between work, the local bar, and her boyfriend's house. Stan would often call the house collect from prison. Every time I heard his voice on the recorded message, I would be transported back through time.

I was married to Danny for a total of four years. During those years I was in a constant state of anxiety. I felt broken and unlovable, so I was constantly seeking signs of betrayal from Danny. We argued almost daily. We ran from his parents and grandparents to my mom, to friends, and for a while we even ran from the Marine Corps because Danny just couldn't handle being a Marine.

I was right to be on guard for betrayal because the final reason for our divorce was Danny's multiple infidelities. Leaving my first marriage became a defining moment in my life. For the first time in my life, I was truly on my own. I was heart-broken but determined that I was going to make the most of the rest of my life.

Despite all the strife that riddled mine and Danny's life together, I am and will always be thankful for the lessons I learned as his wife. We were two very broken and traumatized kids trying to make it work and we simply couldn't overcome the darkness we both derived from.

I was ready to start over. I was ready to brave the loneliness. I was ready to learn what it meant to take care of myself.

In the summer of 2008, I moved back to Indiana. My brother, his wife and two kids, as well as my mom were living in a house in rural Indiana.

I had finally gained some work experience while in Missouri. I even had my own car. I didn't know what the future held, but I was ready to get to know who I was and what I was capable of.

Chapter 47

2008 was a new landscape for many in America. The stock market crash had an impact on everyone's lives. The older generation laid claim that they had warned us of these inevitable trials. How now we would understand what they lived through during the Great Depression. For the first time in our lives, it was difficult to find employment.

I lived in a tiny town in the middle of a small state, in the middle of the country. I had little job experience and only my GED as education. No one was hiring. I spent hours putting in applications in my small town as well as the bigger city twenty miles away. After applying, I would then spend hours calling and checking on the status of those applications.

I finally spoke to the store manager at a local department store. I begged him to give me a chance. He repeatedly told me he just didn't have the hours to give me. I pleaded; I would clean the toilets, do anything, as long as I had a job. I knew if he would just give me an interview, I could convince him that I was worthy of a job. He finally agreed and I got the job. You would have thought this was a powerful office job instead of a part-time gig behind the jewelry counter.

Not only did I get an exciting new job, but I also had a reunion with one of my best friends. Grant and I had worked together briefly at a local furniture rental store near the end of my marriage to Danny. Grant was actually my manager. We had grown close quickly, but since we were both in other relationships at the time, neither one of us ever admitted to the other about the crush that we had had on each other. I came home from Missouri around the week before Christmas. As soon as I walked into the store that Grant worked in, it was like a meet cute in a holiday romance. Grant's eyes lit up and we moved towards each other seemingly in slow motion, as he wrapped me in his arms and spun me around. We were so excited to see one another. I had left several months ago to try one last time to make my marriage with Danny work out and we just simply weren't compatible any longer.

Grant and I discussed how we would love to get together and catch up. I liked Grant a lot. He was smart, funny, incredibly good looking, and he had a job! However, I was still a little leery of any type of commitment. Even just a dinner. So, I asked for him to give me his number instead of me giving him mine. I hugged him and promised I would text him.

The holidays were difficult for me. Stan had been released from prison and my brother had convinced me to go with him to see Stan and his new wife for dinner to celebrate. It was not an enjoyable experience. Stan was incredibly self-righteous. Most of the conversation revolved around his experience in prison, both good and bad. Something that was hard for me to process was that while he was in prison, he received free education as well as free counseling services. Meanwhile, I was on the outside struggling and paying my own way. I left his home that day feeling like all the hard-earned progress I had made was stripped from me.

My brother and I decided that since the dinner with our father didn't go as planned, we would host a New Year's party just for us and our friends. I thought this would be the perfect time to invite Grant out. We could catch up with each other without the pressure of a romantic dinner.

I texted Grant well in advance to invite him. It was a friendly, and flirty, message. I waited patiently for his response. Several minutes went by with no reply. Several hours went by, and still, no reply. Several days went by and there was no reply. I thought to myself, "what in the world is going on?" He seemed so excited to see me. I had always thought since the first time I met Grant that he was just too cool for me. Maybe I was right.

As a last resort, on the day of the party, I decided to stop by where Grant worked while we were out buying supplies. When I walked in the door, Grant looked both relieved and sheepish. As it turned out, in his nervousness of seeing me, he rattled off the first phone number that popped in his head. That number happened to be his ex-girlfriend, who understandably was not keen on passing my number over to Grant. After clearing up the confusion, he agreed to come to the party that night when he got off work.

By the time Grant showed up at my brother's house the party was in full swing. I could see that Grant was hoping for something a little quieter, so I took him downstairs to where my mom had her own little apartment area. I fixed him a bowl of chili and we sat on the sofa to watch the traditional ball drop on TV. We laughed and talked for hours. It was a feeling of belonging that I had never felt with another person. It was exhilarating and scary at the same time. Grant knew the basics of my past but I had yet to share any details with him.

As the minutes began to countdown towards midnight, we began to share with each other our hopes for the New Year. We were both starting out on our own. We were nervous and hopeful.

The clock struck midnight and Grant leaned into me and placed the softest, sweetest kiss on my lips. I didn't know what the next year held, but my heart hoped that Grant and I would be in it together.

Chapter 48

The bright, hopeful light of the new year wore off quickly. I really liked my job. But I had never had to take care of myself. I had never had to make financial decisions or be responsible for my actions and how they would affect my life. Loneliness hit like an anvil in my chest. I began to consume alcohol on a nightly basis. I also had relapsed into not eating.

Grant and I continued to build a friendship. We had established a routine of hanging out and having dinner together a couple of nights a week. Grant was living with his brother as well, so not having a space of our own made spending alone time together complicated. However, every night at 10 p.m., no matter what we had going on, even if I was at the bar with my mom, we called each other to say goodnight.

Those nightly phone calls were a lifeline. On the days where I struggled to make it from one task to another because of the weight of the anxiety I carried, I counted the hours to the time I would hear his signature ring tone on my phone. I was extremely cautious. We both were. We had both come out of very dark places and neither of us were ready for a commitment of any kind. I also wasn't ready to admit I was falling in love with Grant. But his steady compassion and kindness soothed the rough edges of my heart.

I felt as if my soul was in tatters. I thought the farther I ran from the trauma of my childhood, the easier life would become. My mom and

I had pieced together a sort of friendship. We found that if we treated each other as friends and roommates, we could find a compromise of peace. Though she often strayed into the role of mother, I would quickly bristle against her and things would deteriorate. The friendship between us was a toxic environment fueled by desperation and alcohol.

My life became a crossroads of past and present trauma, coupled with terrible coping skills. I was terribly angry. I felt like I couldn't catch a break. My marriage to Danny was supposed to be my happy ending and I was struggling with letting the idea of that go.

It was a long winter.

By spring, Grant had moved out of his brother's house into a sleeping room. It was common in our area for property owners to divide bigger houses into individual rooms to rent out, essentially just bedrooms for rent. This little room would become one of my favorite places in the world. The only catch was that I wasn't supposed to be there. The occupants all had their own rooms with locked doors but shared a community kitchen and bathroom. The tenants weren't allowed overnight visitors, especially women. However, now that Grant had a space of his own, our nightly conversations, more often than not, became invitations and I would find myself quietly tiptoeing into his apartment.

Grant had always been aware of the abuse I suffered growing up, because we had been close friends before I came back from Missouri. Now that we were growing closer, I began to share with him some of the details of my abuse. I really had no choice. It was a common occurrence for me to wake up in gasps of horror with nightmares while sleeping at his house.

For the first time since I had lost Levi, there was someone in my life who held me and wanted to protect me. It was a relief to lay my head on his shoulder and know that there was nothing that could touch me without going through Grant first.

I was falling in love with Grant. Not in the way of movies, where it comes crashing in like a hurricane. But like the tide coming in slowly, wave by wave. When I was with Grant, the tattered parts of my soul felt a little less ragged. But this wasn't a fairy tale, and love alone couldn't fix me.

Chapter 49

Grant recognized the spiral and did his best to keep me anchored. But I knew I was slipping away. I was only sober for the number of hours I had to be at work each day.

I kept everyone at arm's length and refused to let anyone close to my heart. As much as I wanted to be with Grant, I simply couldn't let the relationship progress. I honestly didn't know how much longer I would be alive. After disconnecting from our nightly conversations, I would lay on the sofa in my mom's basement apartment and list all the ways I could successfully usher myself from the continued struggle of trying to get through the day to the silence of oblivion.

I was angry. I thought that the more time and distance I put between myself and the trauma of my childhood the better things would be. I thought I could pack all these memories and wounds away and they would disappear and heal on their own. No matter how far I ran, I was still with me.

I didn't have the financial freedom or the luxury of health insurance to seek mental health care or to see a regular family doctor to receive the aid of a prescribed anti-depressant medication. It was just me facing a storm of trauma and heartache.

I did have Grant. Grant and I were both still very reluctant to commit and intertwine our lives. We were both desperate to be self-sufficient. Neither one of us wanted to be responsible for another person. But we were undeniably falling in love.

I was spending more time at his little studio apartment, even on nights that we weren't planning to stay together. Often I would call him and say "I can't do it. I can't drive home. I can't face anyone." Without hesitation he would say "Come on over, I'll have your grilled cheese ready." I would climb up the stairs to his room, put on one of his t-shirts and climb into his arms.

One evening while laying with my head on Grant's chest, I took a deep breath and decided I would take down the walls. "Grant..." I whispered. "I can't keep doing this. I love you. But I either need to be with you or I need to be alone. It can't be open ended anymore. I know I have a lot of baggage, but I know that I can be a good partner for you, if you give me the chance." Grant lay quietly beside me. The longer he went without saying anything, the further my heart sank in my chest. I got up out of bed, put on my clothes, leaned over and gently kissed his lips. With tears in my eyes, I told him to call me when he had made his decision.

I made it halfway through my thirty-minute drive back to my brother's house when my cell phone rang. When I picked it up Grant spoke two words "Come home."

A few weeks later, the next phase of my life began. Grant and I moved into a small one-bedroom apartment together. We learned how to be partners. Our love grew and so did our friendship. We loved being together. If my day went poorly, I wanted to tell Grant. If I wanted to do something fun, I wanted to do it with Grant. He was my best friend.

The first week we moved in we decided we would take a week's vacation. For the first time in our adult lives, we were both eligible for paid time off through our jobs. We didn't have money for a vacation, but we didn't need a fancy destination. We had a queen size mattress on the living room floor, cheap takeout pizza, and stolen cable from the neighbors. It couldn't have been better if it was a beach side resort.

That's not to say everything was perfect. It wasn't always sunshine and roses. There were times when life reared its ugly head. There were times when life was simply hard for both of us.

I struggled. Honestly, I was so tired of struggling. I loved Grant so much. But I was so caged in by my anger and trauma. I couldn't trust myself or Grant. I pushed him away with all my might. But he stayed. The harder I pushed the stronger he stood.

There were even times when I walked away. But it was never long before I came home. We learned to take this new life day by day.

Not only was Grant loving me, he was teaching me, not just about love and trust, but also how to be an adult. He taught me about work ethic and the importance of giving my best to every job. He taught me about finances and how to manage them, to not only survive, but to get ahead. He even tried to teach me how to cook, but I wasn't particularly good at it.

Slowly the shadows began to grow thinner, and the survival tactics of drinking and self-harm began to slow and even subside.

We were coming up on our first Christmas and soon our first year together. It had been many years since I was living close enough to attend my family dinner on Christmas Eve. I had worked 10 days straight to be able to have Christmas Eve off. I went in to check the schedule a few days before and I was scheduled to work. I marched into my assistant manager's office. I argued and argued. I couldn't figure out why he insisted that I had to work. He finally took me off the schedule. Little did I know the reason I was on the schedule was because Grant had been trying to work Christmas magic behind the scenes. When getting me on the work schedule backfired, Grant had to scramble to come up with a new plan. On Christmas Eve morning, Grant called me while I was running last minute errands and asked me to meet him at the store I worked at to pick up a last-minute gift as a favor for him. I asked him why we couldn't just get it at the store that I was at and he insisted on using my discount. I rolled my eyes and told him I would meet him there. I browsed the aisles as I waited for him. Grant was always late. I heard my name called over the intercom to come to the register. Why were they calling me to the register? I wasn't on the schedule.

As I neared the desk I notice a Santa Claus. He held a dozen pink roses and a wrapped pink box. My face began to blush. By this time all my co-workers had gathered around and I see Grant laughing and beaming a smile from outside the big windows at the front of the store as Santa booms "Grant wants to wish you a Merry Christmas." I accepted the roses and the box. Inside was a pink iPod that Grant had already loaded with all my favorite music. To this day it was one of my favorite Christmas gifts. Not because of the presentation or the expense, but because as I scrolled through the song selection on that little electronic device, I could see how much Grant loved me through the music that he had taken the time to sort through and download. Not only did he recognize how important music was to me, but he had paid attention to hours of music I listened to in order to find my favorite songs from every genre. It was the first time that I had a tangible, physical representation of someone's love for me.

Our relationship kept growing stronger through our first year. We rented an apartment in both our names. We decorated together and bought our first furniture. We began to make financial decisions together and dreams of our future.

One day while walking through the mall we stopped in a jewelry store and Grant casually suggested we should look at engagement rings, for fun. I giggled uncertainly and agreed to try one on. As soon as the jeweler slipped the ring on my finger, I felt my chest tighten and bright red hives popped out on my arms. We both laughed. Nope. Not ready for that.

I knew I loved Grant. I knew he was a wonderful life partner. I even knew chances were good that I wanted to spend the rest of my life with him. But the idea of giving my whole self over to someone again terrified me.

We continued to grow through the next year. We slowly learned that bad days were not going to scare us a way from one another.

I began dropping subtle hints that I was getting closer to the idea of marriage; that I might be interested in a long engagement.

One evening, Grant told me to get dressed, that we were going out for dinner. We pulled up at our local Italian restaurant. The hostess sat us down at a little table in a private corner alcove. On the table were beautiful flowers and several framed pictures of us from throughout our relationship. My heart melted. Grant ordered for us, we ate and reminisced over the last two years and how far we had come. As the server cleared away, Grant pulled out a piece of a paper and began to read a story he had written about me and all I had survived, about our beginning and how we had begun creating a beautiful love story together. The story ended with "stay tuned for the exciting next chapter."

As he read those words, he pushed his chair from the table and knelt on one knee and asked me to marry him. I cried and said yes.

Being engaged didn't change our relationship much. I think it did bring us a sense of commitment and peace. We were growing accustomed to each other and the idea of always being together. We were growing excited for our future. I still had hard days. But now, I also had hope.

Chapter 50

In the summer of 2011, I became terribly ill. I had discovered what I thought was a spider bite on my left hand. As time went on, the bite became increasingly infected. I went to several emergency rooms and doctors and no one could determine what exactly was the cause of the rash or the illness.

I began to complain of being nauseated constantly. I had daily migraines and just generally didn't feel well. I just couldn't figure out what was happening. I spent time on steroids, antibiotics, and even antiviral medications. But nothing helped.

I had stopped working at this point because I was just too sick, weak, and tired. One day I brought pizza to Grant at work for lunch. As soon as I opened the box and the cheesy, greasy smell of pizza hit my nose, I ran to the bathroom. I was so sick. When I came out, Grant was leaning on the wall outside the bathroom and said, "You need to take a pregnancy test." I looked at him like he was crazy. I had been told by a doctor a long time ago that pregnancy was not something that I should count on or hope for. My heart had been broken by a pregnancy test so many times. But Grant insisted. So, I stopped at the store on the way home and picked up a cheap pregnancy test.

I went home and peed on the stick. I didn't even have to wait the recommended time. Those two pink lines lit up instantly. I collapsed on the floor laughing and crying simultaneously. I had wanted to be a mom for so long.

I finally calmed down enough to call Grant, but as soon as I heard his voice the laughing crying took over once more. The only thing I could do was gasp "We have two pink lines!" He also started laughing and said, "I'm on my way home." He then called me five minutes later to remind me I had the car. I drove across town to pick him up.

Within a few days of our positive test, we got in a minor car accident. I went to the emergency room out of an abundance of caution. The baby inside of me was such a miracle, I wasn't taking anything for granted. I remember the nurse at the check-in station told me "Your baby is barely the size of a quarter. It will be fine." I replied that may be true, but to just check anyway.

Grant sat next to me holding my hand as the nurse used the wand to hear the baby's heartbeat. Even before she heard my own, the musical beats of our baby's heart rang out in that little hospital room.

The nurse giggled in surprise and asked again how far along we were. I explained that I didn't really know. I had just taken an at-home pregnancy test two weeks ago. But I had no menstrual cycle to track from as I had never in my life had a routine cycle. I honestly had no clue how any of this worked. I had never been taught about a natural cycle and development of a woman's body.

The nurse informed us that because of how strong the baby's heartbeat came through, she wanted to send us for an ultrasound, "Just for good measure." So, Grant and I waited nervously for the technician.

That night in September we went from hearing our sweet baby's heartbeat for the first time to finding out we were having a boy in just a few short months. I was already four months pregnant and I hadn't even known.

Being pregnant is a challenge. That challenge is further worsened by carrying scars of sexual trauma. Not only for the obvious reasons of examinations, changes to your physical body, and your hormones. But the feeling of not being in control of yourself or the timeline of your life.

Beyond the challenges, there was joy. Grant and I moved out of our studio apartment into a two-bedroom apartment. We spent our weekends shopping at yard sales and flea markets to piece together furniture for a nursery.

We had decided to wait for a wedding so that we could save money for the baby. Life was good and we were excited for the future.

Christmas Eve of 2011 we went out to my Nanny's house for our annual family dinner. I made several comments that I didn't feel very good. It wasn't cramps, I just felt like my stomach was tight and I was uncomfortable. Everybody joked that I had probably just overate, and not to worry. I was only 110 pounds before I got pregnant, so by this time I looked very pregnant, as if I had swallowed a watermelon. I went home and went to bed as instructed by all the moms in my family.

On Christmas morning I woke up still extremely uncomfortable but Grant and I were hosting dinner at our apartment for my other Grandma, my brother's family, and my mom and her boyfriend. I made quite a few comments that I felt like I was having contractions. By the time everyone left that night and I had spent quite a bit of time on my feet cleaning up the mess, I knew that I was experiencing more than false labor. I called the OBGYN and she told me to soak in a warm bath, and if I wasn't better by morning, to come into the office.

The next morning it was concluded that I was in fact in active labor ten weeks early. I was rushed to a women's hospital an hour away, by ambulance. I spent ten days in the hospital on bed rest. I was given medicine to slow and stop labor, as well as medicine to help strengthen the baby's lungs now that he would be arriving early. After ten days it was deemed that if the baby did come early he would be able to stay at our local NICU instead of being at the children's hospital.

After three weeks at home on bedrest and several trips to the emergency room for medicine to stop labor, my water broke. The decision was made for us, the baby was on his way six weeks early. After twenty-six hours and an emergency C-section, Leo was born. We were truly fortunate that despite entering the world on his own timetable, he was healthy. He did spend two weeks in the NICU but by the first of February, we were at home as a brand-new family of three. And thus, begun our next adventure.

Chapter 51

The first few weeks of being home with Leo were exhausting but wonderful. However, I noticed that I wasn't feeling like myself. I would cry for long stretches when Leo was asleep and Grant was at work. I would feel irrationally angry with Grant. I was miserable. Then I would be angry and disappointed in myself for being so sad in what should have been the happiest time in my life.

Of course, with a newborn there were very few hours of sleep. On a normal basis, before the baby arrived, I averaged maybe five or six hours of sleep nightly. Now with a premature baby who needed attended to every two and a half hours, that sleep was cut in half. That not only added to the postpartum chaos that was my emotional state, but it also created the perfect storm for nightmares and flash backs of trauma. Even though the circumstances were different from the trauma I suffered, the emotions, anxiety, and lack of sleep triggered the same fight or flight response.

I recognized how quickly I was beginning to lose myself. I knew that no matter what circumstances I was given, I wanted to break the curse of generational trauma. I wanted to be the mom that I didn't have. I wanted the fairy tale family of grandparents, aunts, uncles, and cousins. However, my relationship with my mom and other extended family was becoming increasingly fractured. I tried to keep the peace with my mom because I desperately wanted Leo to have her in his life.

I reached out to my OBGYN and explained how I was feeling and he was able to prescribe medication to deal with postpartum depression. That wasn't a magic elixir to make life sunshine and rainbows. But it did help me get to a place where I could function and not feel like my world was ending with every inconvenience.

When Grant and I found out that we were pregnant with Leo, I asked for one thing from Grant. That was to be given the freedom to be a stay-at-home mom at least until Leo went to kindergarten. Grant was more than willing to make that dream happen. It took a lot of sacrifice for him to carry the financial survival of our family on his shoulders, but he never hesitated or complained. There were times in the early days of our family where he worked twelve-hour days, seven days a week in a factory to make sure we had our needs met.

When Leo was eight months old we moved into our very first house. We finally had a backyard for Leo to grow into! Like every new family, these were some of the hardest days, weeks, and months of our lives. But they were also some of the happiest. Watching our son grow from infant to toddler, to sweet little boy was one of my greatest adventures. Leo was a bright, mischievous little tyke.

I learned how to be a mother by trial and error. I didn't have anyone to call when there were bumps on the head or late-night fevers. Although my mom was still a presence in our lives, the rift was widening. Now that I was a mother, I couldn't fathom the decisions that she had made. I could never imagine putting Leo in the situations that she allowed for me in my childhood.

I loved being a mother to my active little boy. I loved teaching him and watching him grow. Life was going great. We had our boy, our house, and stable finances. So, Grant and I decided it was finally time to tie the knot. We began to plan a small wedding.

The first thing we needed was a venue. We knew neither one of us wanted to be married in a church. We originally thought we would like to get married in our new backyard. We had set a date for October 30, but in the last two weeks of planning, Indiana weather decided it would like to play a part in our ceremony as the temperature plummeted. There was no way we could comfortably host a ceremony outside when it was only 40 degrees with wind and rain. We scrambled to find a new place to hold the wedding.

At this time, Grant was the store manager for a rent-to-own furniture chain. Some couples get married in beautiful cathedrals, we got married in the showroom that Grant managed. We put sofas and recliners on either side of the showroom to create an aisle to walk down, we hung silver and purple Christmas ball ornaments from the ceiling and used a TV stand and white shag rug to create our altar. For the past few months, I collected baby food jars. We filled each one with white sand and tiny candles to line the aisle. We set up the appliance area with dinettes for our reception. We had a customer who was ordained to officiate the ceremony. She was a sweet lady, but she kept forgetting our names. We also had a customer as our photographer.

Grant had his heart set on being able to buy me an actual wedding dress. He wanted to make this wedding as special as he possibly could. We went to a local bridal shop and tried on dresses. Grant and I didn't have a lot of friends, we knew that we could trust each other, so we kept our circle small and clung to each other. I didn't have bridesmaids. As usual, my mom canceled on me the morning we were supposed to try on dresses. So, Grant took me himself. I found the perfect dress. Poufy, lacy, and $500. The sales lady assured me that we could put $50 down and make payments on layaway. I went to put my regular clothes back on in the fitting room. Staring at myself in the three-way, full-length mirror, I made a decision. It wasn't about the dress I would wear. It was about the life I was starting. $500 was almost a whole month's rent. Instead, we went to a shop in the mall that had Homecoming dresses on sale. I found a beautiful purple beaded gown. I loved it and I felt beautiful. The dress had a long rip on the inside slip. Grant made an offer of $60 for the dress, he went home and stitched the rip up himself. We got the boys matching vests and bow ties at an outlet store. We were thrilled with our little wedding on a budget.

The morning of the wedding dawned cold and rainy. We got to the store early to touch up the decorations. The closest thing we had to a wedding party was two of Grant's employees who stood up with us as a groomsman and a bridesmaid. The ceremony would never make the cover of a magazine, but it was one of the happiest days of my life.

Of course, we couldn't afford a honeymoon. But my aunt Nancy had volunteered to watch Leo overnight for us. When we finally got home that night after cleaning up from the reception, our house was freezing. We had no heat. Our furnace had completely stopped working. Instead of a wedding night consisting of sexy lingerie, we spent the night in layers of flannel pajamas and blankets. It didn't matter. We were thrilled to finally be husband and wife.

Chapter 52

Neither of us had been given solid, healthy examples of how to exist. We had to create our own picture and find our own guides to being spouses, parents, and just adults in general. We were learning how to live and love while raising a son and trying to keep a roof over our heads and food in our bellies. We struggled like every new family. We were determined to not only raise a successful family, but to also find a way to break the cycle of generational trauma.

Each passing year we grew stronger and more stable, both financially and emotionally. We started to find our way and began to lay the groundwork of who we were as a family; outlining our values and beliefs. Things that until this point we had accepted as good practices became cemented to our foundation that we were laying for our son and future generations.

By 2018, life was really good. We managed our own store where Grant and I were able to work together side-by-side at the same desk every day. Leo was in the first grade and doing very well. Our bills were paid and our cupboards were full. But inside I felt like I was drowning. I didn't understand. On the outside it seemed like I had everything I could ever want. And I did. But I couldn't breathe.

The trauma that I had been carrying for so many years was threatening to crumble everything that I had worked so hard to accomplish. I could not carry this burden alone any longer. It was time to seek help from a professional. I had tried several times to seek help through medicine and therapy but had felt that they weren't helping me get to the root of my issues. I had decided that this time would be different. I had learned through being a mother the importance of advocating for yourself. Many times, a medical professional would assume that because of the trauma I had suffered, I must be depressed. And I was depressed, but I didn't have depression. My anxiety was severe and I continued to have what I had started calling "drain thoughts," The thoughts would circle around in my mind the way water swirls around the drain.

I had committed to myself that this time I would speak my heart. I found an amazing psychiatrist who listened to everything I said and she said, "You have anxiety." Yeah, I know. "You have Post Traumatic Stress Disorder." I knew that too. "And you have obsessive compulsive disorder (OCD)." Wait. I didn't count how many times I flipped a light switch or I didn't wash my hands until they were raw. But I did apologize a thousand times a day. I did constantly ask Grant if he was okay. These were signs of very well-masked OCD. As we looked back into my childhood habits, we began to see signs there as well. There was a consistent and insistent stream of thoughts in my mind from the minute my eyes opened every morning until they closed at night. Once I was given my diagnosis, I realized that the constant stream of prayers like "Lord, please protect my family from injury and illness. Please forgive me for anything wrong I have done. Please don't let anything bad happen to the people I love," was in reality, intrusive thoughts and compulsions.

I learned to keep those thoughts and compulsions on the inside. I had been raised in an environment that viewed mental illness in several unhealthy ways. The first one being that admitting to a struggle with your mentality and emotions was viewed as a weakness in your relationship and faith in God. Within our family, any type of behavior that was outside of the boundaries of acceptable behavior my parents set for me was seen as disingenuous and attention seeking. By being taught that these behaviors and feelings were not just immoral behavior but a reflection of my goodness as a person, I learned to mask and internalize those thoughts and behaviors, which in turn worsened my mental illness. Chances are incredibly good that I would have had obsessive compulsive disorder without the added stress of the trauma and abuse I suffered. However, because of that trauma and the inability to express and treat these behaviors, it led to a steady and worsening decline in my mental health.

Finally, after thirty years, I had a diagnosis. I had direction and a plan to follow. By finding the correct prescription, paired with counseling, I was able to quiet the noise and begin to heal the trauma of my past in earnest.

This didn't mean that healing became a beautiful journey of meditation, deep breathing, and essential oils. Healing is messy business. It is still sleepless nights and gut-wrenching sobs. But by controlling the static noise of OCD, I could tune in to the real presentation of traumatic behaviors. Each day became a step in the right direction.

I found ways to channel the darkness. My main goal was to "be who I needed." I tried to find ways in my everyday life when I could be the support and love in someone's life that I needed when I was struggling. Such as buying breakfast for the car behind me in the drive through or giving a sympathetic ear when taking a customer's payment at work.

Another way that I found to heal was by examining my thoughts, actions, and responses to the world around me. When I noticed I was in a situation that made me uncomfortable or caused me to react or behave in a way that seemed outside of my personality, that was a sign to me that I was experiencing something that reminded my body or mind of the trauma. I would then try to take time to sit in those feelings to figure out why I felt the way I did.

The last way I have found to further my healing is by doing research. I listened to podcasts, read books, and articles pertaining to healing childhood trauma and living with my diagnosis. I followed self-help gurus and life coaches on all my social media accounts.

Grant and I talked endlessly about each anxiety attack, every flashback, and weird behavior. Grant would recognize a trauma response and help me overcome it. Sometimes it was something that I had to just grit my teeth and learn to push through. Other things we would eradicate from our life. By doing the work each day, I began to really see hope on the horizon. I could feel myself growing and my life changing.

Chapter 53

The spring of 2020 hit the entire world with a sucker punch in the form of the COVID-19 pandemic. The coronavirus brought about circumstances that most of us had never experienced. Everyone was afraid of getting sick. Restaurants, businesses, and even schools were closed. Life was put on hold. It seemed as if the entire world had shut down.

Our jobs were considered essential because we leased items that people needed such as computers and appliances. Grant and I began to see firsthand how people's lives were beginning to crumble. We also witnessed firsthand, through our own son, how being out of school was taking a toll, not only on his education, but on his mental health as well.

Grant and I began to discuss the situations that many of these kids were facing. The reality was for some kids, school was the only place that they received love and kindness. For some, school was the only place where they had lights and heat, and for many more, school was the only time they had meals and snacks to fill their bellies. We began to imagine how terrible it must be for those kids to be pulled from that building of safety so abruptly and without any answers to what the future held.

It is no secret that child abuse statistics tripled during the pandemic. There were many contributing factors for this. For instance, the levels of stress that parents suffered was at an all-time high due to job loss, lack of childcare, lack of resources, and new fears of illness. This led to higher instances of drug and alcohol use and abuse, which we all know contributes to loss of inhibitions and shorter fuses. That, in turn, can lead to abuse of children and spouses even under normal circumstances.

Many children suffered in silence as well because they were not in front of teachers and school staff trained to recognize their distress. Also, many child protection agencies and volunteers were prohibited from entering homes.

The pandemic created a perfect storm of terrible circumstances for the most vulnerable souls in our communities. We felt helpless but knew that we had to come up with some way to provide comfort to those little ones.

Some of my earliest memories of comfort come from books. I learned to read at an incredibly early age. Even before I could read I would pore over the pictures in books. The idea of escaping my circumstances into a magical realm or some distant land was the kind of rescue I craved. The kids suffering the most during the pandemic didn't even have the luxury of spending hours in the public library, because even that was closed during the nationwide shutdown.

Grant and I decided to call on the power of social media. We posted a request on Facebook that we needed kid's books, teen's books, and coloring books. We began to receive comments and messages by the dozens offering gently used books. We asked those donating the books to put them in boxes or bags on the front porch, then wearing masks and gloves we would pick them up. We took each book and placed them in the heat room we had at our rental store. We let each book sit in the heat at 140 degrees for several hours and then wiped each book down with a disinfecting wipe.

We once again took to social media and asked if there were any kids who could use books to ease their boredom and brighten their day. We had numerous parents contact us. So, we mapped a route on our GPS and took our Sunday off to deliver books around our county.

We knew that we needed to remain socially distanced from these families. And two people walking up to your porch in gloves and masks is scary, so we rummaged around our house to figure out how to be more approachable and less scary while leaving the packages of books on the porch. We also wanted to give the kids something fun to look forward to and break up the monotony of being stuck inside their homes. Our solution? Grant's lobster costume from the previous Halloween. And so, the "Book Lobster" was born.

We delivered books to ninety-two houses over the course of a week. We would bag up several books sorted by gender and age. Shane would take them up to the porch where he would dance a little lobster jig for the kids watching through the window. Then we would wave and move on to the next house.

Were books going to save or change the lives of these families? No, probably not. But hopefully they did go to bed that night with beautiful adventures in their mind, a little comfort in their hearts, and a reminder that they weren't alone in this world.

Chapter 54

Leo was growing like a weed, as they say. I had always heard that the days go incredibly slow, but the years are short. I never understood what that meant until I became a parent. Watching him grow into a funny, bright, and kind little boy was joyful and stressful in a way that only parenting can be.

In many ways, watching Leo grow was like rewriting history. We had story time every day. I rocked him to sleep every night until he was three years old and spilling off my lap. We sang silly songs and played with Play-Doh and finger paint. As he got older we built blanket forts, drank hot chocolate, and watched Disney movies on snow days. It wasn't enough to just not hurt him, I wanted him to know how loved he was every second of the day.

The older he got, the more I began to see myself in his eyes. I saw who I was when I was his age. I recognized my imagination in the stories he told and the games he played. I saw how afraid he was to make a mistake and upset someone. I looked at Leo becoming the age I was when the abuse started and I could feel the remembrance deep in my soul.

Not only did I become hyper vigilant of Leo's surroundings and the people they encompassed, but I also became increasingly aware of the depth and depravity of which my parents had both instigated and allowed to happen to me at that same age.

It wasn't even a question that if anyone threatened, let alone hurt my child, I would rain hell down on them.

But I had a blind spot. My mom. My relationship with her had become the definition of love and hate. The idea of what she had done and allowed not only broke my heart but disgusted me. For the years leading up to this point in our lives, Grant had allowed me to make all decisions about my mom and her presence in our lives. He was always supportive of me and the boundaries that I set, which admittedly weren't many. I always held out hope that she would be different for Leo. Grant was patient throughout the many times that I would rant and cry over my mom letting me down.

At this point in my life, I only spoke to her every couple of weeks and we would go months without visiting one another. But the hold she had over my soul felt supernatural. Cutting her from my life wasn't even a thought that my heart could entertain. It felt forbidden. The idea went against every moral code that had been engrained in me. Like driving the wrong way on a one-way street or placing your hand on a hot stove burner.

I didn't feel as if I had the right to stand up to her. I didn't deserve the freedom of cutting her ties to my life. My mom had convinced me nineteen years ago that her life was destroyed by me saving myself. The little girl inside me took to heart that I owed it to my mom to hurt and suffer because of the chaos I brought about by turning my dad in. All my life, I had internalized the neglect and abuse as something I deserved because of my shortcomings as a human.

Grant did not have a blind spot when it came to my mother. My mom never particularly liked Grant and she really didn't like the woman I had grown into under the nourishing light of Grant's love. Grant was the mask hiding the woman that my mom was from the very beginning. He was cautious in trusting her. However, as Grant and I began to piece together and sift through the past, Grant became convinced that my mother played a bigger role and had more knowledge of what was going on than what she had ever admitted to.

Grant began to question the stories that I had told myself and believed all my life. I couldn't see the truth through the inconsistencies. I couldn't see the forest for the trees. I had told these stories to myself and others so many times in the past, but I never stopped to hear them. Until Grant began to say "Do these stories make logical sense to you? Do you think these were proper ways for a mother to conduct herself?"

I decided that I was going to seek out as many answers as I could find on my own. I began by asking questions of those family members who were around and involved when the abuse was revealed and I was removed from my parent's home. Some family members were more than willing and happy to discuss their recollections, thoughts, and memories with me. Others weren't as forthcoming. Many people asked why I was reopening those doors, not understanding that those doors had always remained open for me. I quickly realized that I needed more than just recollections, I needed as much hard truth and evidence as I could find.

The records from the interviews and observations done by Child Protective Services were sealed, and without a long-drawn-out court proceeding, I couldn't get them released. However, I was able to set up a meeting with the victim's advocate and one of the attorneys from the prosecuting attorney's office in the county where my dad's trial was held.

I was hoping to be able to hear the recorded testimony from the trial. The trial testimony had been recorded on cassette tapes. Unfortunately, the tapes were not stored properly. The tapes had been stored in a damp basement and over the years had become too damaged and degraded to be played. The victim's advocate, however, was immensely helpful and gracious. She did find the case file and allowed me access to as much as she legally could share. There were several things in the file that made a lasting impact; the first was my father's confession.

I sat across the table from the two ladies clinging to Grant's hand with tears running down our cheeks as the victim's advocate read my father's confession word for word. Every letter on that paper detailed the darkest depths of my soul. It was on the paper in black and white. It was no longer some fuzzy, out of focus memory. I heard in his own words the details of what he did, how often it happened, and his absolute confirmation of what he had done. In the confession the detective conducting the interview asked my father "Why?" My father had no answer. In my mind I thought his confession would be simple "Yes's." and "No's," but it wasn't. My father's confession included natural dialog that backed up my accusations with clarity. One comment he made that echoes in my mind was when the detective was asking about the frequency that the abuse occurred. At one point Stan said "Clearly, there were weeks where it occurred more often than others." The casualness with which he made that statement would haunt me. Imagine discussing the way you molested your daughter and stole her very innocence and safety as easily as you would discuss the weather or the local baseball team. He also stated in a way that seemed as if he wanted a pat on the back, that there was a three-week span where he didn't touch me at all. What he didn't disclose was that I was physically five hundred miles away and out of his reach. While listening to his statement being read to me, I had to physically hold myself in place, wrapping my ankles around the legs of the chair, fighting every urge to run from the room.

There were no direct statements from my mother. She was there though. She was there in the minute details. In the way the detective indicated for the record that she would supply a way for Stan to be at the sheriff's office after work. The way that Stan indicated how they had spoken and he had shared every detail with her. And how they were seeking counseling together. All of this once again said with ease and nonchalance. There was no doubt whose side my mom had chosen. It was all there in black and white.

Also in the file was a victim's impact letter I had written to the judge. It wasn't so much what was written in the letter but seeing the signature from my younger self that stopped me cold. I felt so much sadness for the little girl that had signed that letter. I felt more than sadness. There was a small ten-year-old girl inside of me who was cheering in her vindication. The smaller version of myself for once felt validated as the victim's advocate explained how it was noted in the file over and over how my story never wavered. Every interview and statement matched without fail. I may have stood alone, but I had stood strong and brave in the truth.

I walked away from that meeting truly knowing the extent to which my mother knew, understood, and defended the man who had hurt me. I was noticeably quiet on the three-hour ride home. I knew that I could no longer be passive about the role my mom had played and that my relationship with her had to change drastically.

I poured my heart out in a letter to my mother. I asked all the questions that had been buried in my soul for so long. I begged for an explanation, an apology, anything. An acknowledgement of what I had survived and the role she played.

I waited on pins and needles for several days after sending the letter to her by email. Eventually she sent a text message that read: "I read your letter. And I don't know how to respond." That was all she said.

Chapter 55

A Story That Isn't Mine: A Husband's Perspective

It's important as a spouse of a survivor to fully understand that the victim is in control of their story. They are in control of the narrative, the cause and events, and the overall score of the crisis. At no time are we allowed to put our spin on events and tell a survivor what is, or is not correct, or how to feel during a moment of reliving a traumatic event.

However, it is our job as a spouse to ensure the physical, emotional, and spiritual health of the ones we vowed to love and take care of.

At this point, my lovely wife and I have been together for twelve years and married for seven. After having conversations for years about her healing, we started by becoming the people that she needed by creating two successful non-profits. This put her on the track to healing, but only helped her on a surface level. Alice has always been able to hide her true feelings. However, deep down I knew she was still the little broken girl she has always been.

One night in November, we were packing bags for our first charity, and were listening to a self-help podcast. A call came in from a mother who was molested at an early age and didn't know how to deal with the fact that her father who had victimized her, now wished for a relationship. At the end of the call the host said, "If you know he has access to kids you have to report it." Previously, my wife has always said she believes she was the only victim because she was the only one he had constant access to. There was no need to go on the hunt for victims when he had a victim in his own home. However, this night, my wife looked up at me with tear filled eyes and said, "Am I putting others in danger by not saying something to his immediate family?" I responded with a heavy heart, "Yes." It is strange how things come back around. Alice only started to talk about her past when the thought of another being victimized came to mind, just like she did on the stand 20 years ago. I looked up her father's Facebook page and noticed a picture of him and a female grandchild on his lap. The girl looked the same age as Alice when her innocence was taken from her. So, I messaged his current wife.

"Good evening Amelia, my name is Grant. I am the husband of Alice. Please understand that I come from a place of fear. I reviewed some pictures of your lovely family and noticed a small girl that was sitting on Stan's lap. This beautiful, young, innocent girl is the same age as my wife when she was being molested by Stan. I know this is painful to hear but in good conscious and to protect children, I must ensure you know the truth. We visited with the victim's advocate in Ohio who read off the transcribed confession of Stan confessing to engaging in the molestation of his daughter. I'm telling you this because it is now your duty to ensure no other children are hurt by him. I know this is upsetting, however, I could not forgive myself if I knew something and didn't say anything and another child's life was destroyed. I'm sure you don't know the whole truth and I am more than willing to meet with you and show you any proof that you ask for. I assure you that I want nothing more than the protection of children and I hope this message has properly conveyed this. I hope you forgive my abrupt message."

What is interesting is that in the eyes of her family, this wound is healed. I assure you, this is not the case. I later spoke with other family members and the main response I received was "Why are you bringing this back up?" Just because it was over for them, that didn't mean the problem was over with. They don't know about the moments she sits up and screams because our dog's tail accidently touched her thigh while he was rooting around in the blankets looking for a snuggle. They don't know about the moments in the shower when she starts to cry because of a panic attack. The moments that something triggered her past trauma and she travels off in her mind with a blank look on her face. Suddenly,she becomes present and tries to plaster a smile on her face. She tries, however, it is highly unnatural.

I had so many questions that didn't seem to bother Alice. I later found out that she just accepted their truth no matter how inaccurate and deceitful they were. The question that kept running through my mind was why hasn't someone put her healing before everything and everyone else? Looking into the story, I found so many instances where an adult should have stood up and done something. It seemed that those closest to her, the ones that were meant to love and protect her, seemed so absent.

With Alice's permission, I started reaching out and asking the tough questions. Some were receptive, some ignored me just like they did the original problem, and another threatened my life. During this time, I didn't feel like a superhero or felt that I was helping at all. I started this all with the best of intentions and I ended up exiling her family from her. Honestly, I thought with myself curating the conversation that I would finally get the answers she deserved. While we did get some of them, I also started World War III within her family.

With this newly found issue I created, it was now my job to be all the people that took a step back from her when I started asking questions. I was now her mother, brother, aunt, uncle, and grandparents. I took these newly found roles very seriously. I would give her advice in a fatherly way. I would cut up with her like a little brother and get my nails polished at the local nail salon while we gossiped and laughed in a motherly way.

The best way I supported her was by listening. I listened and validated her feelings. I listened to the stories of horrific events and then found examples where she was in a situation that could negatively impact our lives and she did the right thing. For instance, when I was taking apart a bed and the headboard almost fell, which could have caused a light injury to my son, she immediately caught and pushed the headboard back against the wall and yelled out, "Did you know that was going to happen?" Of course, I didn't, however, I took this time to praise her for noticing that something might have negatively impacted our child. She wanted to fully understand all aspects of the event, how to prevent it and, if needed, reprimand me for my careless behaviors.

Most importantly, I learned to be present. When someone is speaking with you about their trauma, it is vital to give them your undivided attention. Make eye contact, pay attention to their body language, talk *to* them and not *at* them. If they are a partner, give them nonsexual gestures throughout the day. This could be as simple as three to five extra hugs. Most importantly, give her unprompted reminders of unconditional love.

During the course of this book, you will see an ongoing trend of adults not stepping up and protecting children. In 2018, 678,000 children were abused in the United States alone according to the Children's Bureau. Every child has the right and deserves to be protected and cared for. I understand that reporting child abuse can seem like a daunting task, however the child may not have anyone else to protect them. Their mental, physical, spiritual, emotional, and possibly their very lives may be in your hands. Please don't wait and hope that someone else does the right thing. Please call the National Child Abuse Hotline at 1-800-4-A-CHILD

Chapter 56

The Sunday night after our Book Lobster route, I crawled into bed exhausted but accomplished. I felt as if we had given the children in our town a small ray of sunlight in a murky world. It didn't take long for us to realize though that we wanted to do more.

What came next would turn out to be one of our biggest undertakings since becoming parents.

We spent much of the next night discussing some of the needs we had discovered as CASAs (Court Appointed Special Advocates), combined with needs we had both had as children growing up in poor, neglectful, and abusive homes. Our first idea was to reach out to children already in the foster care system. However, we quickly discovered that there a charity based in the next county that was already meeting those needs. Upon first learning that, I was admittedly sad. This charity had already done remarkable things and grown past what I could imagine. Where would we fit in? We didn't have a church congregation backing us. We didn't have advisors or even knowledge. We just knew we wanted to help the kids around us. Ever my champion, Grant said we would find the need. And find it we did.

You know the saying "an ounce of prevention is worth a pound of cure?" That became my inspiration. What if we could reach the kids in the midst of trauma, but before removal or disruption? We found that a good portion of calls and concerns coming into the Department of Child and Family Services had to do with absenteeism in school and concerns of cleanliness. We also found that, especially in teens, if children were faced with the idea of attending class dirty, or facing the consequences of failing, they would simply rather not attend and accept failure as the consequence. As someone who was labeled different during my public-school days, this revelation resonated with me greatly. From this knowledge we made the decision to work together with our local schools. By contacting the social workers in our elementary, middle, and high schools, we tapped into the pulse of our children and their needs.

We had the where, when, and why but were missing the how. The how always gives us pause. For any major undertaking, the first thing you need is money. We were just an everyday couple. We lived comfortably, but still lived paycheck to paycheck. We started going through our closets, cabinets, and even my jewelry box. We sold everything we found of value; including auctioning off my Pandora charm bracelet. We did well. But we still weren't quite there yet. We still needed funds for an attorney, licensing, and promotional materials. Not to mention the many things that we couldn't account for because we had no idea what we were doing.

The previous October, Grant had bought me the bed of my dreams for my birthday. A huge king size princess-worthy bedroom suite with scrolled white farmhouse wood, a gray tufted headboard and matching dresser and mirror. It was absolutely gorgeous but we were so close to having enough to start this journey. We looked around the room as we sat on our beautiful bed, and as our eyes met, we knew what we had to do. We sold our bed. We sold our TV. Honestly, we sold anything that was not an everyday necessity or belonged to our son. Grant liked to joke that if I left him, he would get half a mattress. And he hoped it was the half with the crumbs so he had a snack. There was no obstacle too big and no sacrifice too great. We weren't going to take no for an answer.

We finally had the funds. We had the who, what, when, why, and now part of the how. Grant took a crash course at "YouTube University" to help us figure out the basics. We met with an attorney to help us lay the groundwork. Grant taught himself to build a website from scratch. More than just a website, he built an entire framework to track and inventory our donations, where the donations came from, and where the donations went. We stayed up into the wee hours of many mornings learning how to manage and grow a non-profit organization. Now that we knew how to keep track of the inventory, we needed inventory to track. Once again, to Facebook we went. Many people in the community answered the call donating soap, toothbrushes, and deodorant. One day we received a call that became crucial to our success. A lady by the name of Denise volunteered her ability and knowledge of the magic of the coupon world. She would use money from donations and many times our own pockets to buy the much-needed supplies. It was amazing how she could take $50 and double, sometimes triple, the product that same amount of money would normally buy. Her knowledge paired with our fundraising had our spare bedroom filled to the brim in no time.

We would work full time at our day jobs, come home and be parents, and then as soon as our son went to bed, we would stay up extremely late taking inventory, designing flyers, bookmarks, and donation request letters, and packing our bags. We had another amazing community partner step up in the form of a dear friend who worked for a local print shop. Grant took literal scraps of paper from other letters and promotional material we had found online and taped them to a piece of notebook paper and handed it off to Brenda. From that taped up, elementary school looking art project, she was able to piece together beautiful pamphlets explaining our program, letters seeking donations, and our especially important bookmark. It was so important for everything to look professional and she did an amazing job and charged us nothing for her time, effort, and talents. Finally, we were ready. And within a few short weeks, we received our first call and delivered our first backpacks to a local elementary school in our town.

Our backpacks provide children with what they need to be clean, comforted, and ready to learn. We supply toiletries and oral hygiene for every age, and feminine hygiene products for teen girls. Each bag has a night light, regardless of the age of the child that receives the bag. As you know, my room in foster care was in a basement. I was seventeen and embarrassed to admit I was afraid of the dark. I added the night lights to give kids of any age the dignity to sleep in comfort. We supply a comfort item in all our bags, for elementary-aged children, we supply a stuffed animal, and for teens, a soft fleece blanket. Each bag has a journal and pens because every child has a story worth telling. And the most important thing I have added to every backpack is our special bookmarks.

Each bookmark has a list of numbers that they can reach out to, no matter their age, gender, or language. I have even included my own personal phone number. It has yet to be used but I remain ever vigilant day and night.

As of January of 2022, our bags are in twenty-eight schools, including our local Boys and Girls Club, and we have given out 219 backpacks.

Life was starting to run smoothly and we were beginning to find a balance between work, a brand new nonprofit, marriage, and parenting. One night at dinner, Grant was quiet. I said "Whatcha thinking about, babe?" Grant said, "Remember the story about me being a Coca-Cola man for Halloween?" I will never forget this story. This story breaks my heart every time I hear it. My sweet Grant dressed up as a soda delivery man when he was younger. He wore an oversized, red Coca-Cola sweatshirt and jeans that were much too short for his latest growth spurt. He was so proud of himself for thinking of a way to enjoy his favorite holiday without costing his family money. There was no way his family could afford costumes for all three kids. During trick or treating, he stopped at a house where the lady opened the door and smiled and asked what he was supposed to be. When he told her, she curled up her nose and told him "That's not a very good costume." And closed the door without even giving him the longed-for treat.

Grant said, "I don't want any kid to ever feel that way," So, we went shopping for and bought 326 Halloween costumes. In January. And our second nonprofit was born.

On October 31, 2021, we held our first Halloween Party and costume library. The idea was that the children in our community would come to the Boys and Girls Club and pick out the costume of their dreams. They get to trick or treat in costumes they probably wouldn't have otherwise, then return them at one of our designated locations the next day. We then sanitized, repaired, and got them ready for the next year.

We got to see several of the kids who borrowed costumes from us while we were trick or treating with Leo. Each one of them were so excited to show off their superhero, scary monster, or sparkly princess costume and the parents were thankful to be able to enjoy the special memories without the added financial burden.

Many times, throughout this whirlwind year of building and giving, I was reminded of the story of the little boy on the beach throwing starfish back into the ocean that had become stranded by the tide. His father gently explained that there was no way that they would be able to save every starfish. And the little boy replied, "Maybe not, but I saved that one." This also became a guiding tenet for me. Maybe I couldn't change or save the life of every child, but if I reach just one, that would be enough. How different would my life be if I had been someone's one starfish?

Chapter 57

A Letter To Stan

Stan,

This letter has not only been an awfully long time coming but has had to be ripped from my very soul. A huge part of me feels like you don't even deserve my acknowledgement.

I am not sure you are even capable of seeing past yourself enough to ever know or face the reality of what you have done to me. It amazes me how you have moved on and built not one, but three new lives whilst I am here still trying to clean up the mess you have made of mine.

Two weeks ago, I tried to write this letter and my world imploded and I was reminded again how far reaching you have become in my life. I couldn't write honestly. I still wrote with the words and emotions of a tiny, frightened, little girl. Terrified of what consequences would befall me if I exposed you and my true feelings for you.

I am no longer that little girl. She is cradled safe within my heart and I am here to tell you the truth.

I despise you. Contrary to the girl I portrayed to the world for most of my childhood and teen years, I haven't liked you for an exceptionally long time. Not only because of the abuse and havoc you wreaked, but for the manipulative, hypocritical, and narcissistic man that you are. As far back as I can remember you have played the part of an intelligent, upstanding, Christian man. You had many people fooled and still do. But not me. I know how dark and slippery your soul truly is.

You can bluff. You can huff and puff. You can rant and rave. You can insinuate my culpability or threaten me with some imagined dark secret of mine that you think you hold. You and I both know the truth.

I am done. I will not carry your shame any longer. I will no longer sacrifice my peace out of some gesture of protection for you. I have spent the last 26 years of my life trying to sugar coat and minimize the reality of what and who you and my mother were. No more.

I am no longer afraid of you. You hold no power here. I have spent years saying I forgive you. I don't hate you. I wish you peace in your life. Those are lies. Fairly good lies. I even had myself convinced.

The truth is.. I don't. I am angry. You were supposed to love me and protect me from the monsters of the world. Not become the monster. I tried to convince myself that you were only acting out the chaos and trauma from your own childhood. I searched not only my soul but the world over for an excuse for why you did the things you did. But then I realized you created the same chaos in my life and somehow I have found the strength to rise above.

I am tired of tip toeing around pretending that I have something to hide. While you just slide right under and continue living your life as if I don't exist. I am so tired of the "he did his time" excuse. There is no amount of time served that justifies or absolves what you did. You served 4 years. I am currently on my 26th year. 26 years of living in abject terror daily. 26 years of shame and guilt. 26 years of feeling worthless.

Regardless of any excuse you would like to provide, or any irrational narrative you may use. There is no blame to be placed on my shoulders. I was a child.

I didn't fully understand the weight of that statement until I became a parent myself. Being a parent has been one of life's greatest gift. To be entrusted with the opportunity to teach and love a child into adulthood. I will never understand how you so carelessly threw that away.

I have been told by so many through the years that withholding forgiveness is like feeding myself poison and hoping the other person becomes ill. I have and continue to fight that battle and I simply am not able to say that I forgive you. There are some things that I feel can never be forgiven.

I am angry that I must exist in a world where you are present. I am angry that there are still places in my life where I must fear your presence or limit mine because you may show up. I am angry that even to this day …..26 years later I must defend my decisions because you have spent so much time excusing and minimizing what you have done.

This is not anger that inhabits my soul or changes who I am as a person. In fact, the opposite is true. I live my life daily in the light of kindness. I am not a bitter person. I don't want you to think that you have a place in my daily life. You do not. I have refused to allow your darkness to infiltrate the life I have created. The anger I carry belongs to you alone.

I hope that the day comes when you must stare down the dark tunnel of your life here on earth and face every unspeakable action that you made. You do an exceptionally excellent job of keeping your life filled with people, noise, and activity so as to avoid facing the choices you made. But some day you will have no choice but to sit in silence as I have these many years.

For a long time, I have pictured standing at your deathbed reading this letter and finally laying you and all of this down. But with this letter I am doing that now. I am laying you and all the trauma you put into my life down. I have not spoken to you in almost 15 years. But consider this my official and final goodbye. I thought I would grieve. And to some extent I have. However, I realized, I am not grieving you as my father. But rather, I am grieving the idea of a father and all the pretty, fairy tale stories that come with fathers.

I hope that the life you live is kinder to you than you have been to others.

Alice

Chapter 58

Here we are at the end of our journey together. I am so thankful that you have traveled with me this far. Before we part and I send you on your way there are a few more thoughts I would like to share.

Healing is not linear. When someone is healing from trauma in their lives progress is made slowly and one step at a time. Sometimes there will even be days or moments that drag you backwards. Keep moving forward. Even the smallest of steps forward is still a step forward.

I used to think that only once I was healed and whole could I begin to live and experience life. I have learned that this couldn't be further from the truth. It is the living and experiencing of life that brings about healing. Trauma effects more than just our hearts and souls. As science progresses we have learned that when we are affected by trauma we store those experiences in our bodies and nervous systems as well. By allowing the broken parts of our younger selves to experience new emotions and activities in a safe, healthy, and supported environment we begin to reprogram those responses, which in turn allows us to heal.

An incredible piece of my personal journey has been to find places in my everyday life to express and participate in acts of kindness. Ayesha Siddiqi once said, "Be the person you needed when you were younger." This quote burrowed into my soul from the first time I read it. How different would my life have been if the adults in my life had lived by these words? What difference can I make in the lives of those around me, if I began to use these words as the line I measure my life against? I encourage you to ask yourself this same question. What differences can be made if we live our lives from a place of compassion, a place of being who we need?

Kindness does not need to be grand gestures.

In our family we have tried to seek out and create ways to show compassion to those around us. Not just through our nonprofits. But in the quiet, everyday moments.

My personal favorite has been giving away emotional support animals. One day I bought several of the tubes of plastic dinosaurs, farm, and ocean animals from the toy aisle at the local department store. For the next week anytime I came across someone in my daily life, such as a cashier or a server at a restaurant, which seemed to be having a tough day, I would reach in my pocket and pull out an animal. I would hand the animal to the person in need and say " Here is an emotional support animal for you. Keep it in your pocket to help you have a better day." It is amazing how their faces light up with a smile.

My son loves to ask our cashier at the grocery store what their favorite candy bar is. He does an excellent job of pretending to be indecisive and in need of their advice to pick just the right treat. When the cashier asks if he would like his treat now, he replies with "No. it is yours. We bought it for you." Again, to see the faces of these people light up, especially at the end of a long day, is a testament to the impact of even the smallest action.

Grant understands the struggle of being a manager in everyday situations. One of his favorite acts of kindness is to call a manager to our table or by phone to compliment them on the service we received. It has become so common for the only interaction that they receive from a customer to be a complaint that they come to the interaction already defeated. As Grant begins to express how thankful we are for the level of care received, the cleanliness of the establishment, or the deliciousness of the meal, you can see that the person in management begins to stand taller and breathe easier.

It is not these specific acts that are important. There are so many ways to express kindness in our everyday lives. And there are so many ways that kindness changes our everyday lives.

When we begin to view our world from a place of kindness and compassion it changes our outlook. We begin to really see people in their places of need instead of their roles in our lives. I have learned that the most powerful tool in the toolbox for a better world is seeing people for who and where they are. Not their race, gender, religion, job, or who they love. Our greatest need and desire as humans is to be recognized and valued.

As I look back on my journey I see so many times that my life was changed by kindness and other times where it could have been changed with a little kindness.

A call out is an expectation that you have grown, a call on is to hold you accountable for your growth. However, a "call-in" is a call out done with love. A call in is an invitation for growth. That is what I would like to consider this last chapter. A call in to kindness. I am asking that if you take anything from my story it is this: kindness begets kindness.

The word beget is an ancient term, I know. But I love the simplicity of the definition. To beget means to bring about or bring into being. To me that is much more poignant than to simply create or inspire. Each act of kindness brings into being another act of kindness.

Not every act of kindness will change a life. Not every person you are kind to will respond, be inspired, or even be kind in return. That is ok. They are at a different place in their journey.

Kindness isn't just for strangers. We need to learn to love ourselves with this kindness too. I don't mean in the spa day, self-care, and indulgent ways that are so popular in social media. When I say to be kind to yourself, I mean that in the deepest terms.

Love yourself in the way you speak to and about yourself. Love yourself in the way you seek healing. Learn to treat yourself with the kindness and patience you would show a stranger or a friend.

These small acts of kindness, compassion, and even patience alone may not change the world. However, I genuinely believe that if we allow kindness to beget kindness to beget kindness, the ripple effect will build to a tidal wave beyond our imagination.

Find the places in your life, in small everyday moments to be kind. To show compassion. To be to someone the person that you needed someone to be for you.

My hope is that you can take these pieces from the story of the life of a broken girl and use them to inspire hope and change in your lives and the lives of those around you.

Printed in the United States
by Baker & Taylor Publisher Services